AF594126

Human Rights without Democracy?

Human Rights without Democracy?

Reconciling Freedom with Equality

Gret Haller

Translated by
Cynthia Klohr

Berghahn Books
New York • Oxford

Published by
Berghahn Books
www.berghahnbooks.com

Library of Congress Cataloging-in-Publication Data

Haller, Gret, 1947–
[Menschenrechte ohne Democratie? English]
Human rights without democracy? : reconciling freedom with equality / Gret Haller ; translated by Cynthia Klohr.
p. cm.
Translated from German.
Includes index.
ISBN 978-0-85745-786-8 (hardback : alk. paper) — ISBN 978-0-85745-787-5 (ebook)
1. Human rights—Philosophy. 2. Democracy. I. Title.
JC571.H327513 2012
323—dc23

2012024971

British Library Cataloguing in Publication Data

A catalogue record for this book is available from the British Library

Printed in the United States on acid-free paper

ISBN 978-0-85745-786-8 (hardback)
ISBN 978-0-85745-787-5 (ebook)

Contents

Preface

This work strives to bridge a gap between theory and praxis in human rights. Toward the end of my career, I want to pause and connect various experiences to form a coherent whole. Most of the stations in my professional life have, in one way or another, involved issues of human rights; at first from a generally legal perspective, then increasingly in terms of practical application in politics and diplomacy.

A decade ago I began to question the practice of human rights and to share my insights in various publications. Five years ago I began seeking support for those insights by exploring the theory of human rights. It deepened my thought, relativized some of my ideas, and enhanced others.

Nonetheless, my view remains shaped by years of practical experience gained in serving various functions. I now add a critical challenge made possible by having attained a certain detachment.

This work was completed during a five-year stay at the Goethe University in Frankfurt am Main. I owe much to Ulfrid Neumann, who made my stint as a guest professor there possible. He helped me move from the perspective of practical work to that of work in theory and made several suggestions. I also owe much to Klaus Günther, who helped me to access background information and enabled my participation as an associated member in the cluster of excellence program called "The Formation of Normative Orders." Many contacts made in that setting were useful for my work. I would like to particularly mention Christoph Menke, who helped me understand the revolutionary aspect of human rights. Luise Schorn-Schütte helped me better understand John Locke, especially in terms of his own times.

Discussion with Christoph Möllers from the Humboldt University in Berlin helped me not only in comparing national and constitutional law, but also with the democratic aspect of human rights. During a joint course in Alpbach (Tyrol) on the topic of "Human Rights and Morals," Gerhard Luf from the University of Vienna helped me more deeply explore many questions that are important for this work. Heiner Bielefeldt from the University of Erlangen-Nuremberg made helpful critical comments on the manuscript. I thank everyone who participated in valuable discussions there, even the many I cannot list here. Finally, I would also like to thank Maria Matschuk for editorial assistance, Martino Mona from the University of Bern for checking terminology, and Cynthia Klohr for rendering the book in English.

Gret Haller

Part I

THE NOTION OF HUMAN RIGHTS PRIOR TO 1789

The development of what we today call human rights was not linear. Some epochs saw groundbreaking new insights, only to be followed by setbacks. Historically speaking, the idea did not unfold smoothly; some of its meanings developed in parallel, some meanings enhanced, and others contradicted one another. The developments presented in this book do not give the complete picture; they highlight only certain points along the overall emergence of the idea. My emphasis is particularly on those aspects that pertain to specific issues concerning human rights that have arisen in the aftermath of the Cold War.

Chapter 1

THE PREHISTORY AND THE CONTEXT OF HUMAN RIGHTS

More than two thousand years ago, ancient thinkers, too, had notions of human rights. Theirs remained philosophical ideals, however, that were practically irrelevant for everyday life. In medieval times, Christian ideas and, later, the rise of citizen freedom in city-states contributed to the historical development of the concept of human rights but without effecting their actual instatement. The most important growth of the idea began in the seventeenth century. And it was not until the late eighteenth century that the idea of human rights came to be articulated more precisely.

The concept of genuine human rights must be distinguished from the concept of human dignity. Human rights protect human dignity. The first articulation of human rights that emerged in the late eighteenth century meant to do just that. The concept of human dignity had already been around for a long time. We shall take a look at the development of the notion of human dignity first, then, before tracing the philosophical development of the concept of human rights.

The Concept of Human Dignity

Human dignity was an idea familiar to the ancients.[1] The concept had two different meanings: For one, it described a person's status within society. But it also elaborated the value of man in contrast to other species, indicating as it were the intrinsic worth of the human being. At first that dignity was established on the grounds that human beings have the power of reason. Later, in early Christianity and in medieval times, human dignity came to be seen as defining man's place within the overall framework of creation. According to the Bible, God created man "in His own image," making human dignity something derived from a "resemblance to God." During the Renaissance, Italian humanist Giovanni Pico della Mirandola extended that resemblance to imply that man, as a small world in himself, has all the possibilities that exist in the great world created by God and that human dignity consists in having a free choice from among all those possibilities.

With the beginning of modern times and the Enlightenment, the idea emerged that human dignity follows from man's capacity for reason. German philosopher and jurist Samuel Pufendorf said that not only is human dignity based on the human capacity for reason, but that all people are capable of it. This made human dignity the same for everyone.

Philosophers of the sixteenth and seventeenth century began to define the individual's concrete right to freedom based on the idea of human dignity. The labor movement in the nineteenth century made the notion of human dignity the central concept of political struggle, demanding for workers material circumstances "worthy of human existence" and thus adding to the concept yet another aspect, namely, that of what is just. While human dignity remained a philosophical distinction on which to establish human rights, it also began to enter the realm of specific claims to rights, thereby becoming a category of jurisprudence. One example of that transition is the Weimar Constitution of 1919. In the introduction to its passage on the conduct of commerce the Weimar Constitution states that commercial activity must be so organized that it complies with "the principles of equity and the aim to warrant human existence worthy of all."

In response to the unparalleled contempt of human dignity witnessed in World War Two, the preamble to the charter of the United Nations, declared on 26 June 1945, called for "faith in fundamental human rights, in the dignity and worth of the human person." The UNESCO statutes from 16 December 1945 also strove to counter any renouncement of democratic principles and to promote human dignity, equality, and mutual respect. The preamble to the United

Nations Universal Declaration of Human Rights, from 10 December 1948, centers on human dignity. Article 1 says, "All human beings are born free and equal in dignity and rights. They are endowed with reason and conscience and should act toward one another in a spirit of brotherhood."

Anchoring human dignity in this way in international documents eventually makes it a juridical concept, without dismissing philosophical justification for human rights.

Let us now turn to jurisprudential guarantees of human dignity as set down in national constitutions. These make clauses on human dignity a matter of interpretation by the courts. But the debate can get very controversial when such clauses are applied in real-life situations. Some reveal the inconsistencies among diverse interpretations of human dignity. Beginning in the mid-twentieth century and increasingly over recent decades, legal debate over what is meant by human dignity has become part of discourse on how to properly enunciate human rights. Since their first articulation in the late eighteenth century, the struggle to define human rights has never ceased.

Charters of Liberties and the Social Contract

Before human rights were spelled out for the first time, the late Middle Ages saw centuries of development toward what was to become "modernity." In feudal times, people were born into social classes, where they remained—as peasants, craftsmen, nobility, or the clergy—for the entirety of their lives. It was considered an order prescribed by divine provenance. But gradually individualism emerged, especially as people living in cities began participating in municipal decisions. To some extent, it had always been possible to overcome rigid class barriers: sons of peasants, for instance, could enter the clergy when educated for it, or they could become craftsmen and then eventually even become citizens by moving to a city and residing there for a number of years.[2]

The same period saw the emergence of the legal concept of "charters of liberties." One of the oldest known documents describing such liberties, the *Magna Carta Libertatum*, dates from the year 1215. In it the English king agreed by contract to respect certain liberties of his subjects. It was to become a prototype for written constitutions in Europe, written albeit by kings and not by parliaments. The Magna Carta declared that the king could not make certain decisions on his own, but only in consultation with a council of royal vassals. Thus the Magna Carta was a first step toward European parliamentarianism.[3]

Similar documents followed, such as the Petition of Right in 1628, the Habeas Corpus Act in 1679, and ultimately, in 1689, the Bill of Rights, which granted certain rights to the people of England and their representatives. Charters of liberties were historical realities, negotiated and established between rulers and their subjects. These documents did not of themselves question the fact of rule; their purpose was to secure a few customary liberties within the framework of an accepted order. And naturally they could only be drafted on the condition that a state already existed, to which they would then apply.

A charter of liberties, then, differed considerably from what came to be known as the "social contract," a notion of seventeenth-century philosophy. A social contract is not a historical factum; it is an idea, a virtual construct that by definition must precede the establishing of a state. It was pivotal for thought on justice and government. English philosopher Thomas Hobbes (1588–1679) contributed greatly to the rise of the idea. Before Hobbes, the individual was seen solely in terms of his dependence on a divinely prescribed social order, fated to cooperate. If the individual had any rights at all, these followed from a duty toward God and one's fellow men to better oneself and one's existence. Hobbes focused on the individual, who, by nature, is free, and on that individual's rights, which constitute the cornerstone for establishing social order. Such social order could only be secured by surrendering certain personal liberties to the community. That is what Hobbes meant by "social contract."

Basically, the idea presupposes that by nature individuals are born free but that they choose in mutual agreement to establish a political and legal community. It reverses how order relates to freedom. Medieval charters of liberties awarded the individual certain liberties within prescribed class order, their primary goal being to maintain that order. This meant that liberties were awarded only members of a privileged class. In contrast, the philosophical rationale for order based on a social contract addresses the issue of freedom, on which, in turn, order is built. While charters of liberties left existing forms of political power unquestioned, the idea of the social contract re-established and justified political sovereignty by the people.

Inseparably bound to the notion of freedom was the notion of equality for everyone. Historical charters of liberties stated the criteria that individuals had to fulfill in order to enjoy the liberties conferred on them by a monarch. Some liberties applied only to upper classes or certain occupations; others depended on property ownership. Behind the idea of the social contract, in contrast, stands the notion that all men are born free and equal. Since we are all, by nature, born free, we must also, by nature, all be equal. Freedom and equality go hand in hand. If freedom were not bound to equality, we would need some preemptive decision or declaration of who is privileged and who is not, or some criterion for determining who is or is not born free. Such distinctions, however, are not compatible with the theory of social contract, where all men are born free and freedom is not something that can be conferred. Thus one significant difference between charters of liberties and the idea of the social contract is the latter's focus on equality.

Notes

1. See Peter Häberle, "Die Menschenwürde als Grundlage der staatlichen Gemeinschaft," in *Handbuch des Staatsrechts*, vol. 1, §20, eds. Josef Isensee and Paul Kirchhof (Heidelberg, 1987), 834ff.
2. "City air liberates" was the catchphrase. For a discussion of breaking the hold of dominance by religion and tradition, see Hasso Hofmann, "Die versprochene Menschenwürde," in *Archiv des öffentlichen Rechts* (quarterly journal) 1993, 353–77, particularly p. 373 and references. See also Uwe Wesel, *Geschichte des Rechts in Europa* (Munich, 2010), 321.
3. See Wesel, *Geschichte des Rechts in Europa*, 186, 195.

Chapter 2

First Concepts of Human Rights

The idea of the social contract enabled eighteenth-century philosophers to develop the notion of human rights. The following condenses the history of that development, mentioning only those moments of the greatest significance for understanding the concept of human rights. We find such moments particularly in Hobbes, Locke, Rousseau, and Kant.

Hobbes

It was Thomas Hobbes (1588–1679) who first elaborated the idea that social order is not a matter of divine providence. If only in theory, it is up to freely born individuals to create social order. This reflects a transition from prescribed order to an order of choice.[1]

In a prescribed order, liberties can be assigned to specific persons or classes because divine direction determines which persons and classes those shall be and under which conditions such liberties will be granted. Suspending divine order, however, changes the signs. Universal and equal freedom replaces conferred liberties. It is up to humankind to create social order. Since the sixteenth century and Hobbes, mankind has made considerable effort to meet this challenge, and it is still working at it. Hobbes's visionary transition from prescribed to chosen order laid the groundwork for the subsequent development of human rights. Today one might say that the individual is no longer the product, but the producer of social order.

Hobbes thus founded a tangible philosophy of human rights inasmuch as he postulated the birthright of freedom and equality for everyone. But he also had another idea that has been just as important for the development of human rights: Hobbes claimed that in lawmaking a ruler must be absolutely free, responsible only to the community that has authorized him to rule and declare law. It meant the end of rule by divine or natural providence. It presupposed, however, a new authority, namely, the joint authority of the individuals united by social contract—individuals of free and equal provenience.[2]

In Hobbes's plan for society, however, freedom and equality soon become, for the most part, illusionary. Hobbes sought a solution for the seventeenth century's bloody disputes—religious war on the Continent and civil war in England. His concept of the social contract was one way to justify political rule based on individual freedom. But even on his theory, freedom can be precarious; in a theoretical state of nature we would eventually have "war of every man, against every man."[3] For Hobbes the powerful state and the absolute monarch are the solution for law-related uncertainty that is unsettling for society. The people surrender to their sovereign not only the power of legislation, but their freedom and all their rights, too, with the exception of the right to life, which for Hobbes was the only right granted the individual.

Hobbes's arguments lead to absolutist rule. The scheme implies that people can protect their own rights by handing them over to an absolute ruler.[4] Thus for Hobbes freedom and equality exist only within the framework of subjugation. That hardly makes him a human rights theorist. And yet, he did prepare the way for the subsequent development of genuine human rights.

Locke

English philosopher John Locke (1632–1704) took the next step toward more firmly establishing what is meant by human rights. Like Hobbes, who was several decades his senior, Locke started with the natural state of man, where all are free and equal and pursue survival. For Locke survival is not an instinct, but a right and a duty. In *The Second Treatise on Government* he uses the right to survival and the duty to pursue it to justify the individual's right to property, a factor of central importance to his theory.[5] Every individual owns his own person and should therefore own the product of his own labor. The right to property follows from the fact that through labor a person adds something to an object. In the original state of nature, a person also has the right to protect himself from violations of his right, to act as judge toward any perpetrator, and, if necessary, to punish that perpetrator himself. The introduction of money made it possible for some individuals, even in the natural state of man, to work more land than needed for their own subsistence and to sell the surplus in yield. Since industriousness varies considerably from individual to individual, even the so-called natural state knows unequal ownership.

As soon as the individual is no longer in a position to protect "property that extends beyond his own immediate physical strength and control," it becomes inevitable to negotiate a social contract and erect a state.[6] To get that protection, people install a government for the sole purpose of protecting individual rights. By this Locke means the protection of property, which includes one's body, life, and private property. Locke devises governmental institutions accordingly. Through the "Glorious Revolution" of 1688–89 the English parliament had finally limited royal absolutism.[7] Locke took account of these events such that in his theory the legislative process passes from the ruler to a legislative body elected by property owners. He was thus one of the first to broach the issue of the majority vote in parliamentary decision making. It became the task of legislation to pass laws needed for the protection of the rights of the individual, with the enforcement of those laws being placed in the hands of the executive and the two organs being distinctly separate.

Locke's ideas for the design of public institutions sought to introduce favorable conditions for the new upwardly mobile class of economically active citizens. This, among other things, explains his concern with property, which in turn is closely related to the concept of labor. Labor became the legal justification for private property.

Locke also seeks to establish social order based on nature as created by God.[8] Every human being is an independent individual. Nonetheless, he is subject to natural law made by God. Man's main task is to discover and acknowledge the divine law already inherent in nature. Atheists and others that publicly to do not profess God in any form cannot be citizens. However, the ability to recognize laws of nature presupposes a certain amount of education and is thus only available to those who have had the privilege of getting it. It is therefore their duty to accept moral responsibility and share their knowledge with the populace.

Compared to Hobbes, Locke recoils somewhat from the notion of boundless freedom. He reconnects attainable social order to elements of prescribed order and appeals to man's resemblance to God.

But above all, Locke goes beyond Hobbes by devising a different anti-absolutistic scheme that might be called "government by ownership."[9] It alters the relationship between freedom and equality. Under absolute rule, Hobbes had preserved equality by making all subjects equally bound; Locke preserved freedom at the cost of splitting society into the prosperous and the have-nots. Compared to Hobbes, Locke moved the notion of human rights forward by reflecting that the surrender of an individual's rights to the state cannot be boundless. He contributed important ideas for the notion of liberal government by law, which in turn influenced the idea of human rights. But neither Hobbes nor Locke could sustain the promise implied by the idea of the social contract, namely, that all men are free and equal.

Rousseau

It was philosopher Jean-Jacques Rousseau (1712–1778), from Geneva, who seventy years later took on the challenge of that promise and pushed toward the idea of tangible human rights. What counts for Rousseau is not outward law, what counts is inward, namely, the individual's conscience. Rousseau was the first to realize that individual freedom is only compatible with governmental law enforcement when law flows from a legislative process determined by the very individuals that are subject to it. It means autonomy for the individual, or, literally, the condition of being self-governing. Here, for the first time, we also find the individual's double role regarding legal order: The individual has not only to obey the law, is not only subject to it, but is also, along with his coequals, a lawmaker, a coauthor of law. He is both author and addressee of the law. Here freedom takes on a new dimension, namely the right to political participation; every individual is called upon to contribute to the design of public order.

Rousseau's concept for this is that of *sovereignty by the people:* Locke had taken the right to make law from the monarch and transferred it to the parliament; Rousseau took it from the parliament and passed it on to the individuals that constitute the state. The individual, being subject to the law, is only considered free by first consenting to that law, which he does by participating in the creation of it. Rousseau calls the common will of all individuals the *general will;* it is identical with the sovereignty of citizens. Thus the only legitimate law is law that is decided by the people; ultimately this means that legitimate lawgiving is only feasible in moot sessions, in small states. In Rousseau's view the passing of laws by representatives in parliament is incompatible with the principle of self-government.

By refusing to accept authority that lies outside of the individual, Rousseau returned to the idea of individual freedom introduced by Hobbes, but he circumvented the obstacle for the development of human rights that was in Hobbes's way by not surrendering rights to an absolutist ruler and instead transferring them to *the general political will* of all assembled individuals.

Here an element of bondage slips into Rousseau's thought, however, because his handing over of individual rights to the community is just as relentless as was Hobbes's surrendering of them to the absolute ruler.[10] For one, Rousseau transfers all natural rights without exception to the community.[11] Hobbes had at least left us each with a right to life. But for another, the commonwealth constituted by the social contract becomes a unit in itself, with its own will: The rights of the individual blend into it. Once transferred to the general will, individual rights cease to exist.

Rousseau, too, assumed that social order is not something given but that individuals must work at developing a social order for themselves. This considerably upgrades human freedom. Yet at the same time, that freedom is so strongly identified with human perfection and happiness that it seems an almost religious claim to salvation that can easily become totalitarian. Ultimately Rousseau says that a state must guarantee its citizens virtue and happiness. In this radical view freedom practically becomes an illusion.

Nonetheless, Rousseau's attempt to balance liberty with equality and to put both into practice—his notion of self-government and the individual's double role as the author and the addressee of law that he introduces—was, indeed, progress. He had an enormous influence on contemporary political events, especially on the French Revolution. In the centuries that followed his thoughts came to inspire a number of theories, especially radical democracy. And yet, although in the history of ideas his radical work did determine the direction for the further development of human rights, we do not see Rousseau as having founded them.

Kant

One hundred years after Locke, who until then had been the most significant theorist for the concept of human rights, German philosopher Immanuel Kant (1724–1804) from Königsberg took the next crucial step toward a philosophy of human rights, seeking particularly to reconcile freedom with equality. This was clearly a definite move from prescribed to chosen social order.[12] Influenced by Rousseau's thought, Kant used some of the latter's concepts in his philosophy of law, questioning and differentiating them further. Kant took Rousseau's political ideal of the complete merge of the individual with the general will and divided it into a moral ideal on the one hand and a legal ideal on the other. What both ideals have in common is the absence of any concrete content: Kant provides a method for finding, or at least for approximating, the desired content. Both ideals start with individual freedom, but the crucial difference between the two is that while legal directives can be enforced, moral precepts cannot.

According to Kant, man's freedom is predominantly a consequence of the capacity for thought. The capacity for thought puts man in a position to judge and value things and events of the world. Man's power of reason enables him to see what consequences his actions might have for himself and others. But beyond that, according to Kant, in every individual there lies something inexplicable, something that tells him how he ought to behave and whether his actions are seen by both himself and others as justifiable. It belongs to a category that Kant calls moral law. Moral law obligates the individual to do what is right. But whether an individual follows that insight and acts accordingly is up to him; morality cannot be coerced. And even when his behavior is not moral, the individual cannot escape moral law. Whether one wills it or not, the question always arises as to whether one can, in one's own eyes, morally justify a particular action. In Kant's words, what we are dealing with here is the question of whether my behavior is in accordance with my maxim that my acts be such that I can want them to "become universal law," or in other words, to apply to everyone. Relentless compulsion to follow moral law is what Kant calls "the categorical imperative."[13]

Kant does not tell us what is morally right or wrong. What he shows us is how an individual may proceed in order to best determine what is right or wrong. The pivotal criterion for this decision is whether something can be generalized, whether it can be considered universally desirable. It is man's capacity to ponder and decide this—combined with the fact that he is persistently challenged with that task—that imparts upon him what Kant calls moral autonomy. And that moral autonomy is ultimately what defines human dignity. Human dignity is a result of free will. Free will makes us capable of self-governing, or autonomy, when it comes to morals.

Rousseau saw the concept of self-governing as chiefly related to public order enunciated by law. For Rousseau, law and morals are one and the same; within the concept of self-governing he makes no distinction between the two. This approach may have the unfortunate consequence of someone eventually surrendering one's own power to determine what is moral to a totalitarian state. What Kant has done is to separate the two realms, but this does not mean that the individual retains a right to self-government while adopting morals from other instances. It means that when it comes to morals, what we have is not collective lawmaking but individual decision making.

For law, too, Kant focuses on method, not content. The purpose of law is to protect the rights of the individual. Law elaborates the conditions that should guarantee that every individual may pursue and achieve what he desires, as long as it is compatible with the same standard of self-fulfillment valid for everyone. The liberty to do or not do as one pleases is what Kant calls "choice." It includes behavior resulting from wishes, desires, and moods, which, as such, may objectively look unreasonable. But the capacity to choose cannot serve as a foundation for moral autonomy. Moral autonomy flows from the self-governing of each individual under the moral law that is a part of himself and that abstracts from personal desires and fleeting moods. While moral law addresses the individual and leaves it up to each person to deal with it individually, the law of the state governs living together. It protects the freedom of every individual by—if necessary—constraining the liberties of others such that equal freedom applies to all. This again inevitably ties freedom to equality. Freedom can only mean equal freedom for all.

According to Kant, individuals have only "one single innate right" and that is the right to freedom that they have in virtue of the fact that they are human beings.[14] It is therefore also called a "right of humanity" and serves to prevent domination by others. To protect that right, society needs institutions that guarantee the individual's exertion of it. These can only be institutions of the state, and the necessary enforcement of that right must be left up to the state as well.

Like thinkers before him, Kant, too, begins with man in a state of nature. In his version of that condition, things begin with a kind of private law according to which each individual—at least provisionally—may accumulate whatever he pleases. Kant does not see this as ending in a war of each against all; but without some means of legal protection, such a situation will be instable. Thus man's innate right to freedom demands that he abandon the state of nature and subject himself to enforced public law; in other words, as Kant says, individuals must enter a "state of citizenship." People should come together to form a state that Kant defines as "the assembly of a group of people under laws of right."[15]

The duty of men to unite in a state under laws of right, however, follows also from the fact that legislative authority may only be put in the hands of "the united will of the people."[16] Kant adopts Rousseau's notion of the sovereignty of the people, modifies it somewhat, and drops the concept of plebiscitary democracy. In an ideal situation, it would be up to the people, in the name of all citizens, "to procure their rights through representatives." But Kant thinks that this sort of representative system cannot exist until a state has become a "true republic." By "true republic" he means the participation of all citizens in *res publica,* public matters. Thus Kant also calls the right of humanity "the right to a republic," or "the right to government."[17] One of Rousseau's novel ideas, namely, that freedom also involves political participation, now unfolds completely in Kant. Kant lays down the basic components of parliamentarian democracy but discards Rousseau's elements of direct democracy.[18]

Republicanism

Kant does not draft for us a detailed system of state institutions but once again formalizes the issue by showing how one might approximate a republican state. Until a full republican state can be attained, laws must be declared by a monarch with the support of his government officials. That was actually the situation in Prussia, to which Kant's hometown Königsberg belonged. But Kant also kept an eye on the French Revolution, which had broken out in 1789. Convinced that continental European monarchies were in a process of deterioration and that sooner or later the republican state would assert itself, Kant asked how one might devise the transition from monarchies to republics such that violence like that of the French Revolution might be avoided.[19]

A monarch, then, is not entirely at liberty to declare law at whim. According to Kant, a ruler must seek to "declare laws in such a way that these *could* have their source in the combined will of an entire people; he must view each of his subjects … as if that subject had agreed to that joint will. That is the touchstone for the legitimacy of every public law."[20] Here, once again, Kant formalizes the issue; his "touchstone" is a thought experiment. He does not say exactly what is just. Instead, he asks the monarch to imagine whether his subjects would agree to a law, given the chance to do so. As long as citizens are not yet in a position to "procure their right" via representatives, the monarch must consider himself their mandatary and representative and weigh the pros and cons of laws for them. Once the citizens have attained the state of the republic, they can do so for themselves. Kant sees them then also taking the formal route: citizens are not to examine whether laws are pleasing or personally beneficial, but whether a specific law can be willed by all that are subject to it. For Kant the universal will is not the same as the sum of all private interests. Instead, legislation requires that citizens abstract from their own private situation and employ universal rational criteria to examine whether an envisioned regulation can be generalized to apply to everyone involved. Once again, the crucial point is universal validity. By striving for this, the citizen is initially freed from himself—from his own perhaps fleeting and, under objective scrutiny, perhaps unreasonable desires and moods. That is a prerequisite for testing universal validity.

Here the legal sphere meets that of the moral. Moral law, too, constantly confronts an individual with the question of whether his actions conform to a subjective maxim that he "can will to become a universal law," or, in other words, that he can want to be universally valid. And once again, the "touchstone" is a thought experiment. Just as an individual can only justify any one of his actions by asking himself whether it would be desirable that the underlying maxim become universally valid, so too must the citizen, when participating in the shaping of law, ask whether that law would be desired by all that are subject to it. Morally, it is the examining of one's own maxims by applying the categorical imperative to them that reveals individual human dignity. It is analogous to lawmaking: there the sole innate right to universal and equal freedom is revealed when lawmakers examine proposed law in terms of its universality and thereby determine the general will of the people.

Kant's republicanism surpasses domestic borders. Just as individual human beings abandon a state of nature and subject themselves to government by "laws of right," so too should nations strive to jointly achieve an international setting of right. Ideally, a "federalism" of sovereign nations domestically supported by republican constitutions should work toward international law. Kant calls these cooperating countries a "league of nations," explicitly rejecting the notion of one world government or one global state. His notion of "cosmopolitan citizenship" asks for little more than "universal conditions of mutual hospitality" that enable citizens of one nation to travel in other nations with a minimum of protection.[21] Compared to today's expectations, it was a humble beginning. And yet, Kant did move toward a theory of human rights that transcends the mere protection of individuals within their own country.

Besides suggesting that public law govern how citizens live together under one polity and that international law govern relationships among nations, Kant also suggests what he calls "cosmopolitan" law. This law not only determines which claims an individual has toward nations of which he is not a citizen, it also aims to coordinate how an individual can live with all others who are not citizens of his own country. This gives another dimension to the innate right to universal and equal freedom.

Notes

1. Hans Ryffel describes the transition from prescribed to chosen order in *Grundprobleme der Rechts- und Staatsphilosophie. Philosophische Anthropologie des Politischen* (Neuwied and Berlin, 1969), 190. He also sees this transition as one from *mythos* to *logos*, a social and political transition that occurs programmatically in all cultures. See Ryffel, "Zur Rolle des 'Absoluten' in der Philosophie der Politik," 32ff.
2. Thomas Hobbes, *"Leviathan" oder Stoff, Form und Gewalt eines kirchlichen und bürgerlichen Staates*, 1651 [Leviathan, or the Matter, Form and Power of a Commonwealth, Ecclesiastical and Civil (1651)], translated into German by Jacob Peter Mayer, Stuttgart, 2010, 151ff.
3. Hobbes, *Leviathan*, 115.
4. The paradoxical idea of safeguarding rights by surrendering them was around before the notion of human rights emerged. See Hasso Hofmann, "Menschenrechtliche Autonomieansprüche—Zum politischen Gehalt der Menschenrechtserklärungen," *Juristen Zeitung* (1992): 171.
5. Walter Euchner, *John Locke, Zwei Abhandlungen über die Regierung* (John Locke's *Two Treatises on Government* translated into German by Hans Jörn Hoffmann) with an introduction by Walter Euchner (Frankfurt am Main, 1967), 27ff.
6. Jürgen Habermas, "Naturrecht und Revolution," in *Die Revolution der Menschenrechte. Grundlegende Texte zu einem neuen Begriff des Politischen*, eds. Christoph Menke and Francesca Raimondi (Berlin, 2011), 108–49, esp. 99.
7. See also Horst Dippel, "Die Sicherung der Freiheit. Limited Government versus Volkssouveränität in den frühen USA," in *Grund- und Freiheitsrechte von der ständischen zur spätbürgerlichen Gesellschaft*, ed. Günter Birtsch, (Göttingen, 1987), 135–57, esp. 138f.
8. We do not know whether Locke was aware of the contradiction this involves. See Euchner, *John Locke*, 1 ff. (See note 12 below.)
9. Ibid., 34.
10. Sergio Dellavalle sees Rousseau's signing over of individual rights to the general will as even more uncompromising than Hobbes's transfer of them to a ruler. Sergio Dellavalle, "'From Above [top down]' or 'From the Bottom Up?' The Protection of Human Rights—Between Descending and Ascending Interpretations," in *Definition and Development of Human Rights and Popular Sovereignty in Europe* (Council of Europe Publishing: Strasbourg, 2011), 91–113, esp. 104.
11. Jean-Jacques Rousseau, *Vom Gesellschaftsvertrag oder Grundsätze des Staatsrechts* (Rousseau's *The Social Contract* translated into German from the French original from1762) ed. Hans Brockard, Stuttgart 1977.
12. Heiner Bielefeldt points out that Ingeborg Maus was the first to detect this aspect in Kant and make it the theme of her Kant interpretation. See Heiner Bielefeldt, *Kants Symbolik. Ein Schlüssel zur kritischen Freiheitsphilosophie* (Freiburg and Munich 2001), 118, footnote 46; Ingeborg Maus, *Zur Aufklärung der Demokratietheorie. Rechts und demokratietheoretische Überlegungen im Anschluss an Kant* (Frankfurt am Main, 1994).

13. Immanuel Kant, *Grundlegung zur Metaphysik der Sitten* [Foundations of the Metaphysics of Morals] 1785, German Academy Edition, vol. IV, 421. What Kant actually says (here in translation) is: "Act as if the maxim of thy act were to become by thy will a universal law of nature."
14. Kant, *Metaphysik der Sitten* [Metaphysics of Morals] (1797). German Academy Edition, vol. VI, 237.
15 Ibid., 313.
16. Ibid.
17. Wolfgang Kersting, *Kant über Recht* (Paderborn, 2004), 51 ff; Robert Alexy, "Die Institutionalisierung der Menschenrechte im demokratischen Verfassungsstaat," in *Philosophie der Menschenrechte*, eds. Stefan Gosepath and Georg Lohmann (Frankfurt am Main, 1998), 244–64, esp. 255; Hans Jörg Sandkühler, "Moral und Recht? Recht oder Moral," in *Recht und Moral*, ed. Hans Jörg Sandkühler (Hamburg, 2010), 9–32, esp. 21.
18. For a detailed analysis see Maus, *Zur Aufklärung der Demokratietheorie*, 191 ff.
19. Gerd Irrlitz, *Kant Handbuch. Leben und Werk* (Stuttgart and Weimar, 2002), 466.
20. Immanuel Kant, *Über den Gemeinspruch: Das Mag in der Theorie richtig sein, taugt aber nicht für die Praxis* [On the Adage that What Might be Right in Theory is Not Fit for Praxis], Berlinische Monatsschrift [Berlin Monthly Journal] September 1793, emphasis in the original. German Academy Edition, vol. VIII, p. 297.
21. Immanuel Kant, *Zum ewigen Frieden* [Perpetual Peace], 1795. German Academy Edition, vol. VIII, 357 f.

Chapter 3

Human Rights, Morals, and Law

Kant's philosophy of law and morals completes our first exploration into the theoretical background of human rights. Other declarations of human rights were also written up in the late the eighteenth century. These followed from the rise of new nations and from transitions of existing nations into new forms of state and government. Theory came to influence political reality and political reality in turn had an impact on theory. Kant, for instance, commented on political events on the one hand, while on the other he gleaned insight particularly from reflecting upon the French Revolution.

In concluding Part 1, we turn now to issues that emerge when we examine what the theories outlined above meant for the development of the idea of human rights. Some have remained relevant to this day.

Normativity and Reality

Ideal human rights are always related to the reality of life in a negative way. When philosophy defines and articulates human rights, it is always in response to real conditions that are in some way lacking; it is always a response to an awareness of some intolerable violation of human dignity. Philosophies of human rights are reactions to something that is "wrong" with reality when compared to an ideal. Rights are worthy ideals that have not yet been attained.

They are norms against which we measure reality. Those norms describe how things should be. We call the articulation of a state of things to which we aspire but that is not yet manifest "normative." Normativity is a gauge for assessing reality. The norm does not tell us how things are, but how they should be. We compare what "is" to what "ought" to be. Today we might say that every human right that has ever been acknowledged started with one person's sense that "something is wrong here." In the face of adversity, one intuits what might be just or fair. Only humans are capable of imagining this.[1] Human beings can reject things and circumstances because they have free will, which, according to Kant, ultimately constitutes human dignity.

Law is always an articulation of human will. Whether it is a national constitution or a statute for the regulation of traffic, a custom governing private contracts or an international agreement among nations, every law expresses human will. Law codifies the will of a constitutional assembly, the will of a body of legislature, an administrative will, or the will of whoever's responsibility it is to formulate the legal norm in question. Defining a legal norm is a normative act; the human will that it expresses culminates in a desired standard. Words that contain no normativity, that is, that do not express human will, are merely descriptive. That description may or may not be adequate, but description alone does not express human will. Notice the difference between laws of the state and government on the one hand and the laws of nature on the other: Manmade laws are normative, laws of nature are descriptive. Traditional science seeks laws of nature on the assumption that such laws exist and can be understood using human logic. Laws of nature do not prescribe anything; they do not express any will, they simply describe features of nature.

Normativity as it relates to human rights means that we set a standard that does not coincide with real conditions as we find them and that we insist that conditions change to meet that standard. Normativity gives us arguments that justify the demand that an actual condition be altered in order to come closer to a specific ideal. But it also implies that the desire for change must be well founded. A norm must always be backed by a reason, even if in reality few people fully endorse that reason. A norm lacking a justified reason for its existence or validity is not a norm; it is merely an expectation adorned with a claim to absolute validity.

The idea of human rights thrives on the tension between a claim and its becoming reality. As soon as reality becomes the standard for measuring things, human rights lose all substance. In other words: when reality comes so close to our ideals that we can use reality as our standard, we no longer need the norm. A perfect world would need no human rights. History has seen many disastrous instances when, in an attempt to make reality match the ideals, the true circumstances were declared to be or accepted as the standard. Dictators have had to misrepresent and conceal realities in their own countries in order to feign adherence to reasonable standards.

But neither can a norm that is too remote from reality—a norm used to channel life in a certain direction—describe the perfect world. Human rights are always expressed in real contexts and always remain imperfect. It takes an identifiable historical situation and real human suffering for human rights to become a normative gauge of any value. Suffering at other times, in other historical contexts, or in other countries or regions of the world changes the significance of that value. An entirely different case of suffering may add to the under standing of a right or help to make that right more precise. And sometimes subsequent injustices reveal inconsistencies in earlier norms that in their time were in turn responses to previous injustices.[2]

Thus whether human rights are effective depends in two ways on making a clear distinction between claims on the one hand and reality on the other:

For one, a claim to a right must always imply some improvement over a real situation that is considered unfair; any other implication would culminate in an illusion of a perfect world or in dictatorship. Norms and reality are related precisely because the reason for wanting a particular standard is to alleviate some real suffering.

For another, proposed solutions to existing problems can always only be provisional.[3] No claim to a human right is absolute; it must always be expressed in terms of concrete circumstances that exist at some time and in some place. Human rights mean a long-term effort to approximate an ideal, like our concept of human dignity that is never quite perfectly expressed.[4] If we knew how to perfectly articulate that ideal, the process of approximation would be complete: we would have either perfect peace or dictatorial silence.[5] Every declaration of human rights is to some extent "'presumptuous' because it lays down principles and rights that have not yet been (politically) achieved and grants these rights to agents that likewise do not yet truly exist—namely, fully free human individuals."[6] National constitutions are vague answers to such presumptions and sometimes surpass them in declaring human rights. "The promises made by democratic constitutions should not be a constant source of disappointment ... but an incentive to improve the system."[7]

Normativity and Human Rights Theories

The course taken by human rights theory reflects this tension between normativity and reality. We cannot deny that Hobbes's idea of the social contract is a normative starting point for human rights. Hobbes posited individual liberty once and for all. But the reason why in his theory freedom and equality become illusionary is because Hobbes neglected normativity. Instead, his practical outline for society was guided by what he considered to be reality. Hobbes assumed that without constraints, human beings, born free and equal, would eventually find themselves in a struggle of each against all and that the only way to prevent it would be to have a strong state and an absolute ruler. In terms of normativity, Hobbes does not give us liberty and equality; he gives us nothing with which we could lay claim to them. On the other hand, he does give us a normative rationale for statehood, which he sees justified by a superior right: the right to life. In other words, free and equal individuals need a state to guard them from anarchy and demise.

In Locke we see normativity taking the opposite route. Locke's sole normative standard is that of individual rights, in particular, the right to property, which includes one's body, life, and private property. Even in a state of nature, the individual has a right to them. They exist prior to the establishment of the state, and a state may only take on a form that does not violate these rights. Locke's notion of the organization of state and government itself is not normative; its sole purpose is to secure individual rights.[8] His reason for those rights, however, is normative: they set a standard against which to measure any reality that may deviate from them. Because Locke, too, had English social circumstances in mind, his notion of state and government is also informed by the conditions that existed then and there. And since he put the authority to create law in the hands of the legislative body, he must clearly define the limits of lawmaking. Thus for Locke, legislation is constrained by normatively established individual rights that exist prior to the state. The sovereignty of Parliament, as developed through various charters of liberties following the Magna Carta, is the most important feature of the British tradition of human rights. Locke's normativity trusts that constraint. His second treatise on government is an "appeal to the people and those governing them, to design their relations in accordance with that."[9] Locke's normativity provides arguments that defend the individual's right to freedom vis-à-vis the state.

In contrast, Rousseau's normativity focuses on how to best organize governmental institutions, especially sovereignty by the people. For Rousseau individual rights do not exist prior to the state: with its authority to make law, the sovereign populace must first define those rights. Rousseau even stresses the difference between normativity and reality by distinguishing *volonté générale* from *volonté de tous*, which is the sum of all individual interests and wants. *Volonté générale* expresses the normative concept of sovereignty by the people. It is the ideal common will of all individuals subject to the law in question—a law to which they have agreed after having debated the issue democratically. Since it is an ideal, Rousseau can say that the *volonté générale* could never violate human rights—it must always be "on the right track."[10] The actual sovereign, however, may very well go off track and violate human rights, namely, when following the *volonté de tous* and allowing individual interests to gain the upper hand.

Rousseau provides for no constraints for normative lawmakers, not even constraints through individual rights. Individual rights have no normative effect because here the normative lawmaker is identical with the actual lawmaker. Even if the latter were to neglect human rights in lawmaking, the resulting law would be the last word as founded on the *volonté générale*. Ultimately the difference between reality and normativity disappears: "is" and "ought" become one and the same. For Rousseau human rights have no normative quality, they cannot be used as a normative gauge. On the other hand, he does give us normative arguments for demanding participation in policy making. He was the first to express a normative concept of sovereignty by the people, and that was a groundbreaking move toward the development of modern democracy.

Compared to the other three philosophers, Kant's normativity gives us the most comprehensive set of arguments for human rights. In contrast to Rousseau, Kant's crucial step is to avoid making the ideal lawmaker identical with the actual lawmaker. Actual lawmaking can never attain the ideal of the imagined universal will, it can only approximate that ideal and the notions of right that emerge from the *volonté générale*. For Kant, universal will does not depend on a particular form of government. As long as the true republic has not yet been achieved, any ruler is capable of representing universal will because what counts is not who declares law but whether that law is calibrated by the thought experiment that guarantees universal validity. If a monarch, aided by his advisors, carefully performs that thought experiment, he can, according to Kant, help legislation approximate the theoretical universal will just as democratically elected lawgivers would.

But monarchial lawmaking can only be a temporary solution because for Kant republicanism has a normative quality.[11] The republic is the desired form of the state toward which every other form of government must aspire. This makes Kant's arguments normative in two respects: For one, the individual can demand to be involved in policy making; for another, the individual can claim human rights. One cannot exist without the other. For Kant, human rights and political participation—today we would say human rights and democracy—imply one another.

Natural Law and Positive Law

Natural law is a concept of crucial importance for the rise of the idea of human rights. It suggests that we might extract from human nature some kind of moral order that is of significance and value to mankind. To better understand the concept of natural law, we can compare it to what is known as positive law. By positive law we mean the entirety of all legal norms used in any particular community governed by law. The norms of positive law exist because they have at some time been defined in a formal process of lawmaking called positivization. In comparison, natural law precedes or overrides positive law. Natural law is effective without ever having been decreed or issued or articulated; declaration, issuance, and articulation are necessary features of positive law. Natural law is said to be valid prior to any such formal criteria. The doctrine of natural law views nature and human nature as being independent of human will and action, whether it originates in God or springs from the cosmos or comes from "nature."

From ancient times until the late eighteenth century, "natural law" subsumed large parts of the philosophy of law. Over the centuries, the concept underwent change. Besides having roots in ancient philosophy, it also has medieval Christian roots. These two strands constitute what is considered classical, or traditional, natural law. The traditional doctrine of natural law is linked to divine law. It sees in the world a harmony created by God and expressed in nature, and takes its meaning from that harmony. The Reformation, however, advanced an individualistic concept of man. Protestantism no longer needed the church to mediate between man and God, and the binds of feudal social order were eased. In the philosophy of law this ushered in the transition from classical to modern natural law.[12]

Dutch statesman and scholar Hugo Grotius (1583–1645), also known as the codifier of international public law, initiated that transition. He questioned the relation between concepts of natural law and those of divine law.

In 1618, as a consequence of Dutch disputes that were won by the Calvinist party, Grotius was charged with treason and sentenced to life imprisonment on an island. His wife, Maria, and their maid Elsie were permitted to bring him by boat not only food, but also the volumes he needed for his studies. In 1621, after the scholar had spent two years in his cell, the two women smuggled him out in a book crate. Grotius then drafted international law for Europe that later, in 1648, three years after his death, was to seal the Peace of Westphalia.[13]

Although Grotius denied that natural law is bound to divine law, he did believe that natural law had a divine origin based on God's design of man, such that man is capable of inferring valid principles from human nature.

Samuel Pufendorf (1632–94) took the next step to promote the transition from traditional to modern natural law. We need not take recourse to God in order to define norms of natural law, he said, their definition follows from man's reason, instincts, and context.

Other thinkers also elaborated the concept of natural law, moving further away from a concept of divine prescription and toward universally valid and acknowledged values defined by human reason. Human reason replaced divine prescription, thereby secularizing natural law.[14] *Modern* natural law has also come to be known as "rational natural law" or "law by reason."

Yet the transition from theologically founded natural law to natural law grounded in man's capacity for rationality alters nothing of the fact that the doctrine of natural law starts with a "cryptic, prescribed order in nature and society" known only to those who exercise the faculty of reason, in other words, known only to philosophers, theologians, jurists, and other experts.[15] An analogy was seen among natural science on the one hand, which explores existing laws of material nature, and natural law, on the other, which explores the naturally given laws of society. Just as Isaac Newton in the seventeenth century discovered the law of gravity, so, it was thought, one might also discover the natural laws of society. Whereas in positive law all normativity flows from human will, in natural law—which includes modern natural law—it does not. This has to do with the concept of man that underlies natural law.

The underlying concept of man, namely, is an element that throughout the transition from traditional to modern natural law has retained its meaning and remains effective right up to today. Advocates of modern natural law wanted to start with human nature "as it happens to be" and not, as traditional natural law had assumed, as it "ought" to be.[16] Traditionalists wanted to describe human nature as being permanent and unchanging, a notion unwittingly based on the concept of man that was fashionable at the time. Similarly, modern natural-law theorists have also unwittingly allowed contemporary ideas to enter their concept of "the true nature of man," namely, precisely those ideas of human nature deemed necessary for arriving at the principles to which they aspire. This only works "if we first attribute to human nature certain cultural demands and needs and then, like a magician, pull big things out of the hat that we beforehand neatly packed into it."[17]

In contrast to positive law, there is no way to apply natural law; it is only an ideal, or "law in the ethical sense of fairness." That is exactly why it has been so important for the development of human rights. From the start in antiquity until the late Middle Ages human dignity was exclusively a category of natural law. Natural law centers on human dignity and derives from it the idea that an individual person has real claims. Historically, the universal validity of human rights was based on a rationale drawn from natural law because in natural law the validity of human rights does not depend on the decision of any specific community governed by law: in natural law the validity of human rights rests wholly on the fact of being human. Nonetheless, at the end of the eighteenth century, natural law did give the positivization of human rights a certain momentum. It made human rights a code of law, and, following positivization, natural law itself was then substituted by positive law.

The notion of sovereignty is another concept that while initially important for natural law, also eventually induced the abandonment of natural law in favor of positive law.[18] During the Middle Ages the most important tasks of a worldly ruler were military leadership and adjudication in the name of divine law. During the sixteenth century the notion arose that a king ought to be entitled to decree law as he saw fit. A ruler's authority to make law became known as *sovereignty*. The term goes back to French jurist Jean Bodin (1529–96), who sought to reduce political chaos in his country by presenting an order conducive to peace. Religious wars had destroyed social order, ending in the bloody terror of the St. Bartholomew's Day Massacre of 1572, when thousands of Huguenots were murdered at the command of authorities. Bodin defined the state as "the sovereign power to govern in terms of justice." Modeled after the French monarchy, the authority to declare law lay in the hands of the absolute ruler.[19]

Bodin still understood royal authority to make law as being subordinate to higher, divine law. It was Hobbes who abandoned that position. For Hobbes, natural law and sovereignty meant that individual rights flow entirely from the power to create law and the process through which it is done. In other words, Hobbes introduced uncompromising man-made justice in which the only binding law is positive law. Although every individual may do as he pleases, it is also desirable to prevent the war of each against all. This is done by an absolute ruler, who declares law. The ruler is no longer bound to divine order: once the social contract has led the populace out of a state of nature, the ruler is free to create law. Hobbes tied sovereignty to the authority to make law and the form in which law must be articulated in order to be valid. He simultaneously freed sovereignty from all other ties.

Locke and Natural Law

Locke, too, saw the central purpose of lawmaking in the securing of liberty. But much had changed in England since Hobbes. In 1688, during the Glorious Revolution, Parliament had finally asserted itself against the absolute monarchy. Modeled on that situation, Locke's theory sees the parliament as being the sovereign lawmaker. This was a first step toward public sovereignty, although "the public" meant only those citizens that through various charters of liberties had already been allotted certain privileges. But in comparison to Hobbes, here the pendulum swung back to a commitment to natural law. Locke could not take Hobbes's "bold step, intentionally declaring it a task of the state to declare good and evil, thereby viewing moral norms as something fundamentally man-made. On the contrary, Locke wholly rejected the idea."[20] Thus the Enlightenment's theory of natural law seemed inconsistent. On the one hand it was based on the notion of natural harmony created by God, the foundation of classical natural law. But on the other hand, its bearings lay in a new, individualistic idea of man freed from the social bonds of feudalism and striving for personal, individual self-fulfillment in manufacturing and commerce.

In Locke this inconsistency can also be seen in the relation of liberty to equality. His notion of freedom is shaped by the new image of the individual: Locke wanted the best of conditions for the new class of economically active citizens and focused his theory on the liberties of property owners. Yet he used the other extreme, namely natural law, to justify the division of society into the haves and the have-nots. That justification did not only mean that the have-nots must respect the property of others; it also meant that property owners must respect divinely defined order. Like all others, property owners, too, have not only the right but also an obligation to survive. Locke's reasons for liberty are future-oriented, but his reasons for dismissing equality come from the past. He advocated a form of modern natural law that cannot work without taking recourse to classical, i.e. God-given, natural law.

That inconsistency in Locke's reasoning reflects nothing other than the social contradictions of the times. He first assumes a natural equality among all men but then justifies inequality, an inequality that was actually the result of production processes, by arguing for moral natural law. In doing so, he goes beyond classical natural law: "Locke's theory of man, striving constantly to add to what he owns, is one of the theories of the modern take on natural law that erodes the classical theory of natural law from within, without questioning its framework of the existence of God-given natural morals that man is capable of recognizing."[21]

Locke also used natural law to justify the right to resist oppression. This right is a guard against the abuse of authority by both the executive and the legislative organs when these venture beyond the sole purpose of the state, which is to protect the lives and property of its citizens. It was a privilege of property owners alone—those who owned no property had no right to resistance. Once again we see that Locke's rationale starts at both extremes of the epoch's historically inconsistent concept: Locke's thought that under certain circumstances an individual has a right to resistance follows from the future-oriented aim of keeping the liberal development of commercial activity free of intervention by authorities, be that executive or legislative intervention. But he legitimized that right to resistance with classical natural law. Yet in fact, the latter actually only allows resistance for the purpose of reestablishing divine order that has been disrupted: classical natural law knows only restoration. It would be up to modern natural law to abandon the right to resistance and become revolutionary.[22]

Rousseau accomplishes that transition. Like Hobbes and Locke, Rousseau, too, used natural law to establish an innate right to liberty for all. Within his scheme a right to resistance makes no sense because the *volonté générale* is always right, it can never be wrong. Locke believed that natural truths are recognizable by the educated. Rousseau said that virtue is not grounded in higher learning but is livable, above all, by "simple folks." It eliminates the moral responsibility of the educated for the common people. Rousseau took the lawmaking sovereignty that Locke had transferred to parliamentary legislation and handed it over entirely to the people. This was homage to Hobbes, who saw rulers as not bound to any specific content of law and as being beyond any critique from subjects. Rousseau saw the individual liberated from all prescribed content and at the center of legislation. And yet we do see a parallel between Hobbes and Rousseau with respect to natural law. Rousseau took Locke's theory and developed it further in a way that is similar to how Hobbes took Bodin's theory and moved forward with it. Both of them, namely, removed the concept of sovereignty from its previous relation to natural law and law by human reason. This liberates lawmaking from all prescribed content. The difference between these two disengagements from natural law in the sixteenth and seventeenth centuries is that while the step from Bodin to Hobbes pertained to royal sovereignty, the step from Locke to Rousseau pertained to sovereignty by the people.[23]

Kant and Natural Law

In Kant, the way human rights relate to natural law takes yet another turn that we can definitely call the final abandonment of traditional natural law. Kant allows only one right to have a root in natural law, namely, humanity's innate right to freedom.[24] Kant endorses Rousseau's notion that people need not be particularly well educated in order to do what is right. Neither does he see nature as telling us what to do. Nature does have its own order, which it is up to natural science to discover. But nature provides no clue as to how we ought to cooperatively organize our lives; nor can we get any such directives from some cosmic or divine order that may back nature. Kant's focus on human reason and the deriving of human dignity from it does not mean that he considered reason a natural human faculty. He explicitly denies that human rights can be grounded in anthropology.[25] For Kant, mankind has the moral duty to promote the furtherance of reason.

However, Kant does see the regularity of nature, the regularity that natural science explores, as analogous to the strict kind of regularity that must be applied to the thought experiment for determining the universal validity of our principles. He also sees moral law as analogous to laws of nature, because moral law compels us time after time to examine the acceptability of our behavior. His esteem for moral law graces even his tombstone: "Two things, the more often and earnestly we ponder them, fill the mind with ever fresh and growing admiration and awe: the starry heavens above us and moral law within us."[26] It is homage to the tradition of natural law. Although we can draw from nature no specific, practical directives for moral behavior, it is nature that compels each of us, for one's own sake and for the sake of living cooperatively, to continue searching for an order that seems right and justified. Thus Kant gave natural law a new twist, perfecting and modernizing the idea at once.[27]

Nonetheless, we cannot say that Kant grounded human rights on natural law. Kant's "law of reason" is not the law of human nature that came to replace classical natural law. Natural law legitimized by reason still rested on a predefined order of the world that man, because he had reason, was allegedly able to recognize. But because reason is not distributed equally among all individuals, it remained the task of particularly qualified individuals, scholars, and experts to recognize that predefined order. In agreement with Rousseau, Kant clearly rejects that idea. He tells us that when he began his philosophical studies his "deep thirst for insight" led him initially to believe that knowledge and insight alone "constitute the honor of humankind." He sneered at "common, uneducated folk." But reading Rousseau changed his mind: "Rousseau proved me wrong … and I have learned to respect all people."[28]

Kant circumvented the decision between natural law and positive law by saying that human nature is characterized by reason and that it is the task of mankind—through self-governing—to achieve a lawful order through which human reason can articulate itself. For the first time, Kant made it possible in theory to abandon prescribed order, whether divine or natural, and embrace man-made order. The only directive that remains is that of moral law. One might say that Kant made a move from natural law having specific content to natural law in terms of procedure only.[29]

Kant, too, leaves little room for the right to resistance. This is because there is no specific predefined order to which to return when rulers abuse their authority.[30] Kant also shows, once and for all, that no clear universally valid and permanent rights can be deduced from "human nature" itself. "Kant's insight leaves no way back."[31]

On the other hand, Kant did not question the notion of absolutely "correct law," even though law must have varying content for different people at different times. In this respect he says that lawmakers must continually work at approximation to the best law. This task demands of them a great awareness of their responsibility; they must conscientiously perform the thought experiment to determine whether proposed laws can be considered universally valid.

But more than anything, Kant finds an entirely new way to replace a notion that had always shaped the idea of natural law, namely the notion that somehow mandatory items of law might be deduced from human nature. Kant individualizes "what is right" by owning that every single person is capable of the moral autonomy that puts him or her on the path to that process of desired approximation. The process itself is not exhausted by criticizing the current state of things; it also means that the individual is called to actively intervene in politics within given means, although at the time some of those means did not yet exist.[32] Kant challenges every single person to participate. In his view it is the principle of the moral autonomy of every single individual that creates human dignity. Kant's philosophical contribution to the development of human rights was groundbreaking. Its full implications have yet to be realized.

Autonomy, Virtue, and Compulsion

Despite his admiration for Rousseau, Kant does fundamentally differ from him. Both focus on the concept of autonomy, but in terms of how law relates to morals, they come to entirely different conclusions. Hobbes had been the first to basically redefine the value of morals in lawmaking. For Hobbes's uncompromising positivistic law, the only law that holds is that which has been agreed upon in legislation. It clearly sunders statute law from any and all theological morals or philosophical ethics. Today's pluralistic societies cannot ignore this.[33]

How the state is set up is a question exclusively of what makes it work well. Its organization cannot be derived from ethical or philosophical principles. In Hobbes's view, legislation has nothing whatsoever to do with virtue. The sole criterion for what is or is not a valid law is the fact of enactment. Effective law is therefore not "true" or "good," not even "right" or "just." Effective law is simply the body of statutes that can be enforced by state authority. The purpose of law is merely to secure peaceful order in society. It has nothing to do with religion or truth. This was a profound novelty, eliciting almost a "Copernican Revolution in thought on law."[34]

That "revolution" was slow and occasionally stalled. But it had far-reaching consequences. Man was no longer seen as the center of the universe, but as a subject that can stand back and observe the world objectively—from nowhere, as it were. It involved a severing of reason from reality. Reality was no longer simply God's creation, something that man must accept as an immovable fact: man began, by dint of reason, to question things. And ultimately—a point that is vital for the development of human rights—morals and law drifted apart: they were no longer identical. This does not mean that ethical arguments play no role in legislation. Whoever was to participate in determining what is to become law was obligated to consider which moral norms can gain enough support to be cast as law. The task is particularly to examine which moral arguments are recognized so clearly by all that they not only can be accounted for by law, but that they must become law, if law is to uphold its claim to validity.

Locke does not distinguish between law and morals. He does distinguish divine law from law of the state, and these from the law of public opinion and reputation. Each type of law is distinguished by the sanctions that follow violation. Violating divine law is sanctioned in the next world, violating law of the state is punished by the state, and violating the law of public opinion and reputation is punished by scorn. But the difference between the three categories is only one of degree. All three make up the model of order that Locke thinks is exclusively backed by natural law, which is ultimately divine law. The effectiveness of both morals and law by the state depends on the sanctions expected for violating them. Thus the difference between religious, moral, and social norms is not one of principle, but, at most, one of degree.[35] And in the question of how to best organize the state, too, Locke cannot go along with Hobbes's uncompromising denial of any role for moral philosophy. He does make the virtue of the individual in principle a private matter, inasmuch as a lack of it does not unsettle the state. But for Locke the purpose of that state is, above all, to enable its citizens to live in harmony with predetermined natural law.[36]

Rousseau's extreme emphasis on morals ultimately leads to the demise of freedom. For Rousseau political liberty is linked to an ideal of virtuous happiness guaranteed exclusively by a republican state. The individual is asked to completely shelve his private interests and, as a citizen, to get deeply involved in the political community that in turn gives him a new identity. Thereafter the citizen lives wholly for the state and finds his own happiness in the state's prosperity. Self-interest is replaced by patriotism. Rousseau wants a *religion civile*, a religion of citizenship that has much greater implications than what Locke posits as guidance by divine natural law. And yet the creed that Rousseau desires is "purely civilian, … it being the task of the sovereign to define its articles, not as rigid religious dogma, but in the spirit of cooperation, without which it is impossible to be a good citizen and loyal subject."[37] Besides belief in the sanctity of the social contract and the laws, the religion of citizenship is also based on belief in the existence of God.

The difference between Rousseau and Locke is particularly one of freedom of conscience. In order to achieve social cooperation, Locke asks only for outward loyalty to the state that he sees strengthened by religious faith. Rousseau wants loyalty of the heart. The citizen is asked not only to obey the law, but to "earnestly love" it. While Locke believes that religion buttresses law and morals, Rousseau's entire republic is religious. Only a virtuous citizen can meaningfully participate in lawmaking. Law is supposed to be "right," and it can only be so when it expresses the common good. In other words, Rousseau's republic is a virtuous state. Its theoretical conception is totalitarian and was de facto later used to justify totalitarian schemes. Its emphasis on virtue and its enforcement make it totalitarian. Morals and law coincide; they cannot be separated in the way suggested by the Copernican Revolution in thought on law.

Kant, Law, and Morals

Rousseau's political ideal saw the individual entirely absorbed in the jointly articulated common will. Kant split this ideal into two parts: a moral ideal and a legal ideal. This duality still holds. Perhaps we could say that it was up to Kant to clearly see this momentous difference and to complete—as it were—the Copernican Revolution in thought on law that began with Hobbes but had not, or not yet fully, been elaborated by later philosophers. Kant radically separated the two realms: the realm of morals from the realm of law; and then showed how they are related to one another. The most obvious difference, of course, is that legal precepts are enforceable, while moral precepts are not. But Kant's explanation for distinguishing between these two realms also shows why they remain reciprocally referential.

The purpose of a legal system is to regulate the outward organization of living together as human beings. While moral law obligates us to comply with legal norms, our reasons for doing so may vary. We may take moral law very seriously and therefore subject ourselves voluntarily to legal norms. Or we may not blindly believe in moral law but nonetheless find that some legal norm or another makes sense and that we should therefore adhere to it. Or we may find the legal norm inappropriate but adhere to it anyway for fear of penalty. Obeying the law thus says nothing about a person's morality. And, according to Kant, this is as it should be, because the very fact that the purpose of legal codes and their enforcement is to facilitate living together means that these should never in any way attempt to influence the conscience of those subject to them. The results would be disastrous. It would encourage the establishment of Rousseau's virtuous state with its reciprocal lack of trust, its spying and snooping. Inevitably, an inquisitional state that expects a certain ethos of its subjects will use legal sanctions to control attitudes. That is self-defeating, because the extreme control of attitude and thought easily ends in chaos, as we know from the French Revolution. It also threatens morality: it implies that individuals are incapable of following inner moral law. Kant saw these two threats: "Woe to the lawmaker that aims to achieve by coercion a constitution based on ethical ends! He would not only achieve the exact opposite, but undermine and destabilize his own political intentions, too."[38]

The contrast between the realm of law and that of morals brings out another difference, namely, the difference between obligation and entitlement. For Kant, every duty is a moral obligation, for the simple reason that it is derived from moral law (an inner sense of what is right). Whether a moral obligation becomes a legal duty depends on the legal setting. Violating a lawful duty will be penalized, while violating a mere moral obligation goes without recognizable sanctions. The positivization of rights that changes them from being morals to enforceable law obscures obligation and puts entitlement in its place. The fulfillment of a moral obligation is voluntary; one who is merely morally entitled has no right to demand anything. A beggar may hold out his cup to a passerby, but whether or not he gets alms is a matter of the other's conscience. Moral order thrives on compulsion; in morality the prime agent is the individual with a sense of what is right. But things are entirely different in law, where the prime agent is a legally entitled individual. Someone who claims a right to which he is entitled "by law" forces the other party to respect that right. We thus have a shift in perspective when moving from morally felt claims to positive entitlement. "Agents take up a different stance when, instead of asking for compliance with moral notions, they start claiming rights."[39] While moral order flows from a sense of obligation, legal order rests on rights.[40] A person who feels morally obligated will choose his own behavior; in legal systems it is the entitled person who can influence or even decide how the other party must behave.

The sense of what is morally right is not only important for whether individuals comply with legal norms; it is an important component of the legal system itself. Morals constitute the normative rationale for laws; our moral notions are what law articulates. The lawmaker, be it—as in Kant—a monarch in a pre-republican state or the representatives of an active citizenry in parliaments of republics, does nothing other than try to translate moral expectations into law. The thought experiment for testing universal validity that Kant says we must use in order to discover whether a law can be desired by all subject to it does not refer to the private interests of those subjects. Instead, the question is to be posed in terms of the universal will and answered using universal criteria of reason. Kant thus in effect makes the moral law within us the foundation of all law.[41]

But the attempt to translate moral codes into statutes always remains an unfinished task. This, too, follows from the Copernican Revolution in thought on law that opens our eyes to the fact that the justness of law and the enforcement of law are not one and the same. Instead of claiming that our legal precepts are just, we achieve a continual approximation toward what might be just, but what that is remains something we can never exactly define. As a result of the Copernican Revolution in thought on law it became obvious that law is man-made and can never be absolutely correct, true, good, or just. Whether we think we can create such law remains a matter of belief. The Enlightenment put lawmaking not only in the hands of humans, but also in their heads and hearts. To ask that that law be absolutely "right" would come close to blasphemy, because we would be equating man's product with the work of the divine.

But in Kant the process of approximating what is "righter" is also driven by the moral law that lies outside of the institution of law. Just as our moral sense time and again compels us to do what is morally right, moral principles themselves have the tendency to induce their "manifestation in a constant process of enlightenment, in other words, legal sanctioning," or to become law.[42] Thus morals have a twofold effect on law: Moral law commands the individual to adhere to legal norms. It also challenges the community to translate moral norms into positive law with sufficient support and recognition. We can even detect a third duty that is prior to the codification of law, namely, man's moral duty to abandon the natural state in the first place and unite as citizens subject to legal statutes. It is man's innate right to freedom from which we derive that duty.

Kant names no specific criterion for the distinction between moral norms and legal norms except the formal criterion of enforcement. Taking an issue or claim from the realm of morals to that of positive law thus also acts as a filter: Norms that fail to pass through the filter (for instance, because their underlying moral conceptions are controversial and insufficiently supported or acknowledged) simply remain moral norms and do not become enacted law.[43] As a result, that issue or claim will not be regulated by law, in other words, the moral norm will not be enforced. This protects the individual's autonomy when it comes to that issue, protecting the individual from both legal coercion *and* moral expectations.[44]

Law Facilitates Morals

One function of law, then, is, as it were, to relieve the individual of the burdensome aspect of morals. Liberated from moral constraints, the individual may do as he pleases, as long as that behavior is not forbidden by law. What Kant calls free choice reaches as far as it does until it collides with the free choice of others. The task of the legal system is to guarantee each individual a freedom that enables him to have free choice and, if necessary, to uphold that freedom with force. Within the scope of that freedom, an individual may even choose not to follow moral codes, because the struggle with morals is a personal one—it cannot be coerced. This does not mean that we may not discuss our moral views with others. To the contrary, discourse is helpful for shaping one's own idea of morals. But in contrast to lawmaking, just discussing moral norms does not lead to any general commitment to them. In the system of moral values, it is always up to the individual to decide where he stands, in terms of both content and his willingness to abide by them.

When we consider that the individual is both the author and the addressee of legal norms, we see just how law can relieve him of the burden of formulating morals. As coauthors of law, individuals are asked to abstract from their own private interests and to use general criteria of reason to examine whether a planned regulation can be considered universally valid by all involved. It is the expression of the moral law that lawmaking must always strive to approximate and that demands of the citizen that he bring forward his moral views. But once statutes have been defined and become valid, the citizen switches roles, from that of coauthor to that of subject under the law or addressee of the legal system. It means a shift in perspective. Being governed by the law liberates the citizen from constantly reconsidering what might be morally right. Of course, nothing prohibits him from further deliberation, but if he wishes, he may limit himself to simply complying with the law. His may be the standpoint that as coauthor of the law he has done his part once and for all and will thereafter simply abide by the law. Certainly, as a citizen he will be called upon to coauthor laws time and again. But nonetheless, once he becomes the addressee of statutes, they ultimately relieve him of a certain moral responsibility.[45]

The individual needs this relief if he is to have the freedom necessary for coauthoring law. In order to be able to abstract from his own personal interests during the process of lawmaking, the individual must take recourse to universal criteria of reason. He must be able to rest on the moral principles that have been previously scrutinized in terms of universal validity. No one can relieve a person of choosing his own moral principles; each must make that decision alone, even after discussing views with others. And when participating in lawmaking, an individual should also be free of moral pressure exerted by others; he should be in a position to submit his own true opinion. As a coauthor of legal norms each individual needs the freedom that the legal system guarantees him as its subject, if he is to develop his own moral opinions at all. He should not have to submit for consideration moral views that others have forced upon him. Moral autonomy, which for Kant ultimately constitutes human dignity, thus also depends on legal autonomy—on the freedom guaranteed each individual by the legal system. Ethical or moral autonomy and legal autonomy mutually entail one another. "For the sake of moral autonomy, an individual must have the legal right to escape the intrusion of authoritarian or governmental moralizing and, if necessary, to hide behind that right."[46] The fact that the compliance to moral norms cannot be accomplished by force enables the individual to freely contribute his ideas to the shaping of societal order.

For human rights it is vital to understand how morality and law depend upon one another, particularly in the interplay of moral autonomy and legal autonomy. Every human right starts, namely, with one person questioning not only what others around him consider "normal," but what they actually take to be a moral necessity. An individual notices that the moral conceptions of his environment do not match his own. And when faulty moral norms have already found their way into legal statutes (which is often the case when the majority considers them "normal"), that individual will believe that these laws need changing. Ultimately, an inexplicable intuition that "something is wrong here" is at the bottom of individual human rights long before they find their way into legal articulation. The difficulty of explaining this feeling is comparable to the difficulty we have in explaining Kant's notion of moral law. It is an inner sense that "compels" the individual to struggle with moral issues time after time.

Every novel way to think about certain human rights begins with *dissidence*. Sometimes it can be dangerous to articulate such thoughts. Morally rigid societies like theocracies have little tolerance for dissidents, and fear the spread of undesired thought. Here lies the key to the transition from Rousseau to Kant. By separating law from morals, Kant allowed for freedom of conscience. Law liberates its addressees from state authority over morals and guarantees its subjects the freedom they need to develop their own individual consciences, a feature that is important if they are to contribute to shaping law. Kant takes the same philosophical step in at last overcoming natural law, both classical and modern. First he overcomes the dogmatism of classical natural law, namely divine prescription. Then he overcomes modern natural law that "unduly blends moral and legal demands."[47] For Kant, truth has no predetermined content; only man's free will can, with increasing accuracy, continue the search for what is right.

On the one hand, according to Kant, moral law demands of the individual that he adhere to legal directives. But at the same time the inner moral sense encourages dissidence. Thus here the citizen has a dual role. Civic identity is always "a combination of allegiance and critique."[48] Moral law demands that the individual who is subject to law adjust his behavior to the latter, while at the same time calling upon him (particularly as coauthor of that very law) to remain a watchful, persistent, and insistent dissident. Clearly, this kind of autonomy is a purely formal concept that must remain open. It cannot have its content prescribed from the outset. From this kind of autonomy (the personal definition of one's own morals) there arise various issues that necessarily compete with one another. This, in turn, keeps the process of regulation going and is—as we would say today—what characterizes social pluralism. But legal autonomy, too, is a purely formal concept. Effective law must constantly be renegotiated, and those negotiations reflect social pluralism.

In closing this chapter, I would like to make one more remark on Kant's thought that law in part relieves individuals of some aspects of morals. The true republic, namely, does not depend on virtuous citizens. In *Perpetual Peace* Kant says that even "a bunch of devils (if they had reason)" could successfully set up a state.[49] Even people who exclusively pursue their own personal interests can make the transition from a natural state to a civilized state, and they need no attitude of common welfare to do so. A person desiring to defend his property and personal interests will—if he is rational—also want society to pass from the natural state to the civilized state, because only then can he live with others "under rules of law" and legal protection. For that period of transition, however, Kant does think that we need moral law for orientation, although there may be free-loaders like that bunch of devils that help to establish a state and constitution for purely egoistic reasons.[50] Once the state has been organized such that its citizens can live under its laws, those citizens may begin introducing their own interests into the lawmaking process. This process may prompt them to discover an attitude of common welfare, because without performing the thought experiment to ascertain the universal validity of their proposals, they will hardly be able to communicate for the purposes of lawmaking. But they could get by without it. Kant thinks that even if in the public negotiation of law people were to pursue solely their own interests and dispense wholly with moral argument, it would still be possible to set up a constitution such that proper democratic negotiation would still necessarily take shared interests into account.[51] Or, as Kant says about the devils, "The outcome will be the same, as if they did not have such sinister intentions."[52]

Notes

1. It is irrelevant for the issue of human rights whether certain animals have analogous capacities, but this does not mean, of course, that we should not protect the integrity and dignity of animals.
2. Menke and Raimondi stress that it must remain possible, in the name of human rights, to normatively alter standards that were previously backed by human rights. Menke and Raimondi, *Die Revolution der Menschenrechte*, 9.
3. See Lefort, "Menschenrechte und Politik," 253–78, esp. 276f.
4. Ryffel, "Zur Rolle des 'Absoluten' in der Philosophie der Politik," 38f.
5. Carl Schmitt's theory shows how mixing normativity and reality ends in dictatorship when the legitimate sovereign of a state comes to power under excep-

tional circumstances, such as the collapse of constitutional order. As Hitler's prized lawyer, Schmitt used this theory to legitimize National Socialism's takeover in 1933. See Müller, *Die demokratische Verfassung*, 136f. (note 4).

6. Francesca Raimondi, "Introduction to Chapter 2," in *Die Revolution der Menschenrechte*, Menke and Raimondi, 99.
7. Christoph Möllers, *Das Grundgesetz. Geschichte und Inhalt* (Munich, 2009), 11.
8. Heiner Bielefeldt, *Neuzeitliches Freiheitsrecht und politische Gerechtigkeit* (Wurzburg, 1990), 65.
9. Dieter Grimm, "Europäisches Naturrecht und Amerikanische Revolution. Die Verwandlung politischer Philosophie in politische Techne," *IUS Commune* (publication of the Max Planck Institute for European Legal History) Max Planck Institute for European Legal History: Frankfurt am Main, 1970: 120–151, esp. 135.
10. Rousseau, *Vom Gesellschaftsvertrag oder Grundsätze des Staatsrechts* [The Social Contract (1762)] Brockard (Stuttgart, 1977), 30.
11. Ingeborg Maus, *Zur Aufklärung der Demokratietheorie. Rechts- und demokratietheoretische Überlegungen im Anschluss an Kant* (Frankfurt am Main, 1994), 148 ff.
12. The term "classical natural justice" is also sometimes used as the generic term for both forms, namely, for both traditional and modern natural justice. Here and in the following I use "classical" to denote traditional natural justice alone.
13. Uwe Wesel, "Die neue Weltordnung," *Die Zeit*, 25 July 2001.
14. Arthur Kaufmann, Winfried Hassemer, Ulfrid Neumann, *Einführung in die Rechtsphilosophie und Rechtstheorie der Gegenwart* (Heidelberg, 2011), 48; Hasso Hofmann advises against using the term "natural justice," because it makes debates confusing. Hasso Hofmann, "Zur Herkunft von Menschenrechtserklärungen," *Juristische Schulung* (1988): 841–48, esp. 843.
15. Marcel Thomann, "Rechtsphilosophische und rechtsgeschichtliche Etappen der Idee der Menschenrechte im 17. und 18. Jahrhundert" in K. Kroeschel (ed.), *Gerichtslaubenvorträge*, Festschrift for Hans Thieme (Sigmaringen, 1983), 73–83, esp. p. 75.
16. Walter Euchner, *Naturrecht und Politik bei John Locke* (Frankfurt am Main, 1979), 26f.
17. Max Ernst Mayer, *Rechtsphilosophie* (Berlin, 1922), 27. Less polemically, Klaus Günther calls the same procedure "projecting [ideals] into 'nature' or the intelligible world," thereby concealing implicit authorship. Klaus Günther, "Diskurstheorie des Rechts oder Naturrecht in diskurstheoretischem Gewande?" *Kritische Justiz* 27 (1994): 470–487, esp. 479. For various reasons why these conceptions are no longer acceptable, see Georg Lohmann, "Menschenrechte zwischen Moral und Recht," in *Philosophie der Menschenrechte*, eds., Stefan Gosepath and Georg Lohmann (Frankfurt am Main, 1998), 62–95, esp. 77.
18. Kaufmann, Hassemer, and Neumann, *Einführung in die Rechtsphilosophie und Rechtstheorie der Gegenwart*, 54f.
19. Jean Bodin, *Sechs Bücher über den Staat*, first French edition dated 1576, German translation edited by Bernd Wimmer and Peter Cornelius Mayer-Tasch (Munich, 1981), 89.

20. Euchner, *John Locke*, 43.
21. Ibid., 43f. On the question of whether or not Locke was aware of this inconsistency, see Euchner, *Naturrecht*, 1ff.
22. Grimm, "Europäisches Naturrecht und Amerikanische Revolution," 120–151, esp. 120.
23. This is pointed out by Hauke Brunkhorst, "Menschenrechte und Souveränität—ein Dilemma?" in *Recht auf Menschenrechte. Menschenrechte, Demokratie und internationale Politik*, eds. Hauke Brunkhorst, Wolfgang R. Köhler, and Matthias Lutz-Bachmann (Frankfurt am Main, 1999), 157–75, esp. 165.
24. Ingeborg Maus, "Freiheitsrechte und Volkssouveränität. Zu Jürgen Habermas Rekonstruktion des System des Rechts," *Rechtstheorie* 26 (1995): 507–62, esp. 541 and 548.
25. Kant, *Grundlegung zur Metaphysik der Sitten*, 1785 [Foundations for the Metaphysics of Morals], German Academy Edition vol. IV, 425.
26. Immanuel Kant, *Kritik der praktischen Vernunft* [Critique of Practical Reason], 1788, German Academy Edition, vol. V, p. 161.
27. Heiner Bielefeldt, *Kants Symbolik. Ein Schlüssel zur kritischen Freiheitsphilosophie* (Freiburg and Munich, 2001), 68f.
28. Immanuel Kant, *Bemerkungen zu den Beobachtungen über das Gefühl des Schönen und Erhabenen* [Remarks on Observations on the Feeling of the Beautiful and the Sublime], 1764, Autograph Remaining Papers, German Academy Edition, vol. XX, 44.
29. Maus, *Zur Aufklärung der Demokratietheorie*, 158. More precisely, Maus calls this a switch "from material natural law to procedural natural law," seeing in it a "Copernican Revolution in thinking in terms of natural law."
30. Ibid., 64ff. For the right to resistance that only makes sense in terms of charters of rule, see 136ff. See also Ingeborg Maus, "'Volk' und 'Nation' im Denken der Aufklärung," *Blätter für deutsche und internationale Politik* 5 (1994): 602–12, esp. 604.
31. Kaufmann, Hassemer, and Neumann, *Einführung in die Rechtsphilosophie und Rechtstheorie der Gegenwart*, 59ff.
32. Gerhard Luf, *Freiheit und Gleichheit. Die Aktualität im politischen Denken Kants* (Vienna and New York, 1978), 64. See also Bielefeldt, *Neuzeitliches Freiheitsrecht und politische Gerechtigkeit*, 124.
33. Claims Hasso Hofmann in "Auctoritas, non-veritas, facit legim?" in *Souveränität, Recht, Moral. Die Grundlagen politischer Gemeinschaft*, eds.Tine Stein, Hubertus Buchstein, and Claus Offe (Frankfurt am Main and New York, 2007), 19–24, esp. 20. Hofmann translates Hobbes's Latin phrase as meaning that laws are made not by what moral philosophers believe to be the truth or what "hairsplitting commentators interpret into a law" but simply by what governmental authority says is the law.
34. Hofmann, "Menschenrechtliche Autonomieansprüche," 165–73, esp. 167.
35. Bielefeldt, *Neuzeitliches Freiheitsrecht und politische Gerechtigkeit*, 57f.
36. Euchner, *Naturrecht und Politik*, 209.
37. Rousseau, *Vom Gesellschaftsvertrag oder Grundsätze des Staatsrechts* [The Social Contract (1762)], Brockard (Stuttgart, 1977), 151.
38. Kant, *Die Religion innerhalb der Grenzen der bloßen Vernunft* [Religion within the Limits of Reason Alone], 1793, German Academy Edition, vol. VI, 96.

Kant calls all laws that are not laws of nature "moral" laws, using this as a generic term to cover both "judicial" laws and "ethical" laws. See Immanuel Kant, *Metaphysik der Sitten* [Metaphysics of Morals], 1797, German Academy Edition, vol. VI, p. 24. Ingeborg Maus points out that Kant calls "ethics" what we today call "morals." It is that terminology, she believes, that obscured twentieth-century reception of Kant's ideas on the relationship between law and morals. See Maus, *Zur Aufklärung der Demokratietheorie*, 326.

39. Jürgen Habermas, "Das Konzept der Menschenwürde und die realistische Utopie der Menschenrechte," *Deutsche Zeitschrift für Philosophie* 3 (2010): 343–57, esp. 349.
40. Jean-François Kervégan "Gibt es moralische Rechte?" in *Recht und Moral*, ed. Hans Jörg Sandkühler (Hamburg 2010), 49–61, esp. 59. See also Jürgen Habermas, "Zur Legitimation der Menschenrechte" in *Das Recht der Republik*, eds. Hauke Brunkhorst and Peter Niesen (Frankfurt am Main, 1999), p. 386–403, esp. 387.
41. Luf, *Freiheit und Gleichheit*, 53ff.
42. Hofmann, "Menschenrechtliche Autonomieansprüche," 167.
43. Maus, *Zur Aufklärung der Demokratietheorie*, 331f.
44. Peter Niesen, "Legitimität ohne Moralität. Habermas und Maus über das Verhältnis zwischen Recht und Moral," in *Zwischen Recht und Moral*. Neuere Ansätze der Rechts- und Demokratietheorie, eds. Peter Niesen and René von Schomberg (Münster, 2002), 16–60, esp. 56.
45. Jürgen Habermas, *Faktizität und Geltung. Beiträge zur Diskurstheorie des Rechts und des demokratischen Rechtsstaates* (Frankfurt am Main, 1994), 147: "In their roles as addressees, the legal system withdraws from legal persons the power to define criteria for judging what is just or unjust. In terms of how justice and morals complement one another, the parliamentary procedure of legislation, the institutionalized practice of court decision-making, and the professional effort of legal doctrines that define regulations and systematize decisions all mean that the individual is relieved of the cognitive burden of forming his own moral judgments."
46. Bielefeldt, *Kants Symbolik*, 111.
47. Luf, *Freiheit und Gleichheit*, 56.
48. Bielefeldt, *Neuzeitliches Freiheitsrecht und politische Gerechtigkeit*, 124.
49. Immanuel Kant, *Zum ewigen Frieden* [Perpetual Peace], 1795, German Academy Edition, vol. VIII, 366.
50. Peter Niesen, "Volk-von-Teufeln-Republikanismus. Zur Frage nach den moralischen Ressourcen der liberalen Demokratie," in *Die Öffentlichkeit der Vernunft und die Vernunft der Öffentlichkeit. Festschrift für Jürgen Habermas*, eds. Klaus Günther and Lutz Wingert, (Frankfurt am Main, 2001), 568–604, esp. 585.
51. Ingeborg Maus interprets Kant in this way in "Freiheitsrechte und Volkssouveränität," 507–62, esp. 562.
52. Kant, *Zum ewigen Frieden*, German Academy Edition, vol. VIII, 366.

Part II
HUMAN RIGHTS FROM 1789 TO 1989

The history of the development of tangible human rights must be distinguished from the historical development of the philosophical concept of human rights. A first major breakthrough for real rights occurred in the late eighteenth century when for the first time human rights became positive law. There were other milestones along the way in the historical development of human rights and some struggles led to codification. As in Part 1, the emphasis in this chapter is on issues that were particularly significant for how human rights came to be treated after the Cold War ended.

The question is not whether human rights are "moral" or "legal" rights, whether they go from being the one to becoming the other, or whether they continue to exist as moral rights after having been codified as legal rights.[1] For present purposes, we shall simply assume that moral considerations may be one source of human rights, just as religion or philosophy may be sources of them. We shall also assume that diverse reasons from all these areas may enter into the process of positivization. More important at this point are the procedures used to turn claims of rights into positive law. And two things must be kept apart: codifying rights is one thing, applying those rights in individual cases is another.

In the following the term, "*positivizing* fundamental or human rights," designates a purely legal matter: it means the converting of an idea into valid and applicable law. The term says nothing about what that idea involves, nor why or whether it may be well founded. It especially does not imply that prior to positivization any particular "moral right" already exists that needs merely to be given a legal form, without changing its content. That would throw us back at least three hundred and fifty years, to how things were before the Copernican Revolution in political and legal thought.

Chapter 4

FROM HUMAN RIGHTS TO POSITIVE LAW

Human rights are universally valid. They hold because we are human, no matter when or where we live.

Historically speaking, by the late eighteenth century the time had come to codify human rights as positive law, to make them rights to which individuals could put claim, though those rights were not yet affirmable in courts of law. The grounds for this move were taken from natural law. While classical natural law permitted only the right to resist oppression for the purpose of restoring lost order, writers of the Enlightenment felt that modern natural law had "revolutionary thrust."[2] With unparalleled fervor, the human right to autonomy asserted itself—an autonomy that literally means giving oneself laws by which to abide. The central document to reach for autonomy in Europe was that of the French *Déclaration des Droits de l'Homme et du Citoyen*, adopted on 16 August 1789, by the National Assembly, during the French Revolution. Its first article: *Men are born and remain free and equal in rights*, "rang like a fanfare throughout Europe."[3]

The very title of the French Declaration of the Rights of Man and of the Citizen from 1789, with its mention of both man and the citizen, mirrors a certain conflict that is inherent to the positivization of human rights. Not only has this dilemma remained unresolved in the past, but it will remain inseparable from human rights for all time.[4] Yet of all of the declarations of rights that preceded it and of all that were to follow, none except the French declaration explicitly addresses this problem: Human rights are universal, but codifying them can only be done by nations. Each nation in its own time, in its own manner, and with its own priorities goes about codifying rights. These rights, however, having thus been codified in different nations, then only apply to the citizens of those nations. The positivization of human rights, in other words, is a matter of geography and therefore means abandoning the ideal of universal validity when it comes to their practical assertion. But this does not mean that they lose their theoretical claim to universal validity.

The French declaration covered a number of rights granted the citizens of France, but it also had an impact outside its native land. It was considered a political agenda, a proclamation of philosophical insights into law that had accumulated over a period of decades and whose time had now come. The National Assembly was believed to have heralded "truths for all times and all nations."[5] But ultimately the French declaration could declare these rights for French nationals only. More than a century would pass before there would be any universal guarantee for those rights. Thus the codification of human rights took place in two general phases, with outcomes sometimes contrary to the original intent: At first human rights were nationalized—and, in practice, lost every claim to universality. Later, in practice, they were to become internationalized and their claim to universality reestablished.

Nationalization

The first declaration of human rights to be formally ratified by a political body was the Virginia Bill of Rights, on 12 June 1776. It was followed by similar bills in other colonies, which were later to become parts of the United States of America. The reasons brought forward by the American colonies for the declaration of human rights differed from those that led the French to revolution. The point in America was to become independent of British rule and to establish a new nation. The slighted British called the events in America a revolution and the Americans rebels and traitors. Americans saw it as a justified war of independence, not a revolution.[6] The Declaration of Independence, signed on 4 July 1776 by representatives of the thirteen colonies, renounced loyalty to the British Empire and made the colonies into states. Some of these states adopted the passage on human rights from Virginia's declaration.

Following the Articles of Confederation, the second constitution of the United States, that in 1787 established one nation with a single president for all, contained no list of rights. In 1789 Congress passed ten amendments, the Bill of Rights (not fully ratified by all states until 1791). The United States of America became the first country to have constitutional jurisdiction.

Although the political background of the American and the French revolutions were clearly different, these two events did have an impact on one another, and this was to a great extent a matter of personal relationships. In 1777, in Paris, Benjamin Franklin, co-author of the American Declaration of Independence, negotiated France's recognition of the United States as an independent nation. Franklin remained America's ambassador to Paris until 1785. Thomas Jefferson, one of the main authors of the Declaration of Independence, followed Franklin as ambassador to France and in 1789 (to the extent that diplomacy allowed) advised various members of the National Assembly in working out the details of the French Declaration of the Rights of Man and of the Citizen. Thomas Paine, an influential Englishman, propagated radical ideals of liberty in both America and France. The Marquis de Lafayette, the commanding general of French forces that had supported the American struggle for release from the British Empire, used the American declaration as a model when writing the first draft of the declaration of human rights for the National Assembly.

The American Declaration of Independence addressed humanity in its entirety—being written, as it were, for mankind. It begins: "We hold these truths to be self-evident, that all men are created equal, that they are endowed by their Creator with certain unalienable Rights, that among these are Life, Liberty and the pursuit of Happiness. That to secure these rights, Governments are instituted among Men, deriving their just powers from the consent of the governed … "[7] But just as in Europe, in America, too, it was impossible to make rights universal. Not only were basic rights reserved for the citizens of the newly founded country, they did not cover slaves. Neither was there any mention of equality before the law; a neglect that displeased even some of the founding fathers. Native Americans were not entitled to human rights—a flaw that went unnoticed for a very long time.[8] It was characteristic of the times that none of the rights documents mentioned women. Their time had not yet come. In 1793 Olympe de Gouges, who in 1791 had proposed and written the Declaration of Woman's Rights and of the Female Citizen as an amendment to the French declaration, was punished for her progressive courage with death on the scaffold.

In contrast to North America, where the people sought to build a new nation, in France the struggle was to renew a longstanding nation from within. The third class, namely the bourgeoisie, saw liberty in disempowering the first and second classes, namely nobility and the clergy, and in appropriating the state. The bourgeoisie was triumphant on 17 June 1789. Earlier that year a threat of national bankruptcy had compelled King Louis XVI to call together an assembly of representatives from all three classes, an assembly that until then had not gathered since 1614. Louis hoped that the representatives of the three parts of society would solve his money troubles, but they disappointed him. On 17 June the representatives of the bourgeoisie declared themselves members of a national assembly. Some representatives from nobility and the clergy joined them, and together they swore not to adjourn before adopting a constitution for France.[9] France's first constitution thus came into effect on 3 September 1791, and the assembly disbanded by the end of the month. The first part of the French constitution is the Declaration of the Rights of Man and of the Citizen.

These revolutionaries were at first swayed by events in America. Leaders in Paris had originally wanted to include the king in the constitution, similar to the inclusion of the president in the American constitution of 1787. But the revolution took a different turn. It became "the first revolution in the meaning of the word as we know it today."[10] The French Declaration of the Rights of Man and of the Citizen actually sparked the next political and social revolution and became its agenda. Jean-Jacques Rousseau's radical ideas especially added momentum. But that same radical and redemption-promising thought eventually led to moralism and the bloody reign of terror under the Jacobin Club. Extreme violence throughout Europe cast a shadow on the French Revolution. Yet the horror did not prevent the revolutionary ideas from decisively shaping Europe. Some of Immanuel Kant's work was written in direct response to that fright.

Nineteenth-century National Positivization

The early nineteenth century quickly lost sight of human rights.[11] The American Bill of Rights became practically worthless; it was not ratified in the states of Massachusetts and Connecticut until 1933.[12] Even the French Napoleonic consulate constitution of 1799 failed to mention human rights. The French Revolution ended with Napoleon's empire overrunning Europe with conquest campaigns. After defeat, in 1815 the Vienna Congress resolved to balance power in Europe. Former order was to be restored and measures were taken to suppress revolutionary activity. Europe returned to a system of monarchies, eliminating all interest in constitutions that might have defined human rights. Of all places, France, the cradle of revolution, returned to monarchy.

But the genie was out of the bottle. Although the 1830 July Revolution in Paris failed and the monarchy was rescued, the latter was given a new form under "citizen king" Louis Philippe and ratified by Parliament. In 1848 revolutionary ideas once again surged in France and spread through Europe. Some countries opted for constitutional monarchies. Some of the constitutions written at that time mentioned individual rights but without aiming for universal validity—they addressed only the rights of nationals. Even in nineteenth-century France, revolutionaries called merely for *droits des citoyens*, despite the much older declarations of 1789 and 1791 that called for *droits de l'homme*. Not until 1946 did the French constitution return to explicitly mention human rights.

Nonetheless, a relatively modest list compiled in 1814 came to be known as "French rights" and became a model used by both the constitutional monarchy of the Netherlands in 1815 and for the constitutions of various separate German states that were written between 1818 and 1833. Norway's constitution of 1814 included a similar list. In Belgium the "Rights of Belgians" were put at the head of the Constitution, placed even before the regulation of duties and privileges of the king and the Parliament. The French constitution of 1848 did not last for long; it ended in a coup by Louis Napoleon, nephew of the former emperor, who was crowned as Napoleon III. The charter of 1814 was also a model for the constitution of Piedmont-Sardinia, which was written in 1848 and would later become Italy's constitution. Switzerland, the only country to have a successful revolution in 1848, gave itself the constitution of a democratic federal state. Even its forerunner, the Swiss Confederation (a group of loosely confederated states that had been recognized as such since the Peace of Westphalia in 1648) had known no monarchy. In 1848 the Swiss Confederation adopted the fundamental rights that individual cantons had in part written into their republican constitutions after the revolution in July 1830, in Paris.

The Fundamental Rights of the German People were written into a constitution negotiated at the Church of St. Paul, in Frankfurt in 1849, but they never became effective, because the King of Prussia vetoed the founding of a pan-German nation. That same year the Danish National Assembly ratified a constitution that included a list of rights. In 1864 Greece took a huge step forward by adopting a catalog of fundamental rights that extended much further than any other in Europe. Further north, in 1849/50 the King of Prussia forced a modest list of "Rights of Prussians" upon his subjects. In 1867 the Emperor of Austria declared the "Basic Constitutional Law for the Rights of Citizens" and created a federal court for the arbitration of citizen complaints of violations of their "political rights guaranteed by the constitution." It was to become the first constitutional court on the continent. The second was created in 1874, in Switzerland, although it made no provision for examining whether federal law infringes on fundamental rights. The Constitution of the German Empire of 1871 made no mention of fundamental rights; instead, it referred simply to promises made in the constitutions of the individual German states.

We cannot here explore in depth how fundamental rights became positive law in the nineteenth century. We turn instead to the dissolution of huge multiethnic empires such as the Hapsburg Empire, Ottoman Empire, and the empire of Russian tsars. In the late nineteenth century a process of disintegration began that was to have lasting impact on human rights in Europe. Before the First World War, new nations such as the Balkan States and Turkey arose within Middle Eastern Europe. After 1918 more new Eastern European nations followed. These states desired national sovereignty and political rights for individuals, though these were often conspicuously nationalistic. The decomposition of formerly multiethnic empires, their falling apart into several new nations, ushered in an unfortunate situation that led to catastrophe for human rights right down to the close of the twentieth century. As the name implies, within multiethnic empires people of diverse cultures had found a way to live peacefully side by side. One way was to encourage local government; another was to forcefully suppress animosities between peoples. Ironically, the struggle for human rights is inseparable from establishing and reestablishing nations. While it went well for the

United States, France, and some other nations, for regions of former multiethnic empires it led to the emergence of a new phenomenon, namely the use of ethnic, i.e., racial criteria, to define nations. Before then no real attempt had been made to homogenize ethnic groups; it would have made little sense. The fragmentation of multiethnic empires in these regions opened the gate for genocide.[13]

These new nations took the shape of either republics or constitutional monarchies, sometimes balancing the two. Fundamental rights found their way into their constitutions, though some were later capped or omitted entirely—a custom that peaked during periods of fascist rule. In favorable cases, constituent assemblies democratically authorized by a country's voting male population articulated which rights they considered fundamental. That articulation was not necessarily preceded by revolution, as had been the case for France. But formulating fundamental rights in assemblies has always been accompanied by a revolutionary spirit and the awareness of building new political order.

Monarchs unwilling to accept constitutions preferred to quell all revolutionary spirit. They sought ways to account for the needs of upcoming commerce without fulfilling republican demands. The solution was to decree constitutions that included certain guarantees of fundamental rights. Because they were issued from the "top down," these rights were naturally retractable. But, for example, some German state constitutions conferred upon subjects by their respective rulers did contain clauses stating that those constitutions could only be altered with the consent of representatives of the people.[14]

Twentieth-century National Positivization

The twentieth century can be seen as the time before and the time after 1945. The main phase of codifying fundamental and human rights occurred after 1945. But in retrospect, the October Revolution of 1917 meant a turn in the human rights movement that was to become particularly relevant for the time after 1989, i.e., after Communism collapsed. Within Russia and later the Soviet Union the positivization of fundamental rights had almost no effect for fifty years. But outside of the country, the Third Pan-Russian Soviet Congress's declaration of the "rights of the working and exploited class" made in January 1918 was, indeed, heard. One year later the Weimar Constitution included the phrase "humane existence" in its wording; humane existence had become an inevitable issue for the industrialized times.[15] Although Russia's revolutionary declaration of rights became a farce under Communist dictatorship, one cannot deny that once it had been articulated, it did acquire programmatic significance.

After heated debate over the legal nature of fundamental rights and how to protect them, for the most part, the Weimar Constitution of 11 August 1919 recapitulated ideas that had already been expressed by the assembly at Frankfurt's Church of St. Paul but that had not become law. It made them more democratic and socially relevant. The long second part of the Constitution was titled "Fundamental Rights and Obligations of Germans." Despite its wording, it did not exclude non-Germans from those rights. It also meant to further just social order.[16] The rise of National Socialism ended that attempt. Throughout Europe fascism soon began abrogating fundamental rights, first in 1922 in Italy, then in 1933 in Germany, in 1936 in Greece, in 1939 in Spain, and eventually in all countries occupied during the Second World War. After the war, many West European countries were able to return to the constitutions they had had before. But Greece, Portugal, and Spain did not do so until the 1970s, when their dictatorships ended.

West Germany's constitution of 23 May 1949 begins with a list of fundamental rights. Because of the unparalleled violation of human dignity and human rights resulting from National Socialism, the constitution's very first article safeguards human dignity. Furthermore, the creation of a constitutional court enabled the updating and extension of fundamental rights through judicial interpretation. Since then, the constitutional clause on human dignity itself has been used in numerous decisions by the Federal Constitutional Court as grounds for enhancing fundamental rights. When the parliamentary advisory council deliberated the German constitution, two different positions emerged concerning what grounds justify human rights. Those who saw National Socialism predominantly as a deviation from Christian morals sought to justify human rights with arguments from natural law. The idea was to rediscover a universally valid standard that had always been there in natural law. The other side found justifying human rights with natural law intolerable because they believed that the act of anchoring human dignity in basic constitutional law must reflect a deliberate democratic decision. The debate needed no settling, for the wording "human dignity is inviolable" permits both views.[17] German constitutional law sees human rights as the fundamental rights that apply to every person irrespective of nationality. Civil rights, in contrast, are those fundamental rights that apply to German nationals.

In France fundamental rights entered the constitution of 1946, but only in the preamble, where they were once again called *droits de l'homme*.[18] It remained that way in the Fifth Republic designed by De Gaulle in 1958, for which he introduced a constitutional advisory council (the *Conseil constitutionnel*) upon which he as president could call if the Parliament should pass laws that are incompatible with the constitution. In 1971 the *Conseil constitutionnel* suddenly decided, contrary to all doctrine, that its right to scrutinize law also applied to the preamble. In doing so it created a kind of constitutional jurisprudence to protect fundamental rights. In order to be effective, however, it had to kick in prior to the final passing of law.

Russia's constitution from the year 1936 became a model for fundamental rights in the constitutions of Middle Eastern European countries that after the Second World War were to become the Soviet Union's satellite states. Outwardly it contained an impressive list of fundamental rights that was purely propagandistic in intent and that stressed participation in public welfare. The list is grotesque in light of the Stalinist terror that lasted until 1953 and in light of all subsequent violations of human rights there.

Colonialism is another factor that we must consider when discussing the development of human rights. In the nineteenth century the countries of South America sought independence from their respective mother countries, choosing either constitutional monarchy or to be republics. But for other colonized continents the momentous move to independence did not happen until late in the twentieth century. Then decolonization led to the formation of new nations. In 1945, 51 countries founded the United Nations. By the end of the 1980s the UN counted over 160 member nations. The importance of decolonization for the assertion of human rights reveals more irony and bitter truth: Well into the nineteenth and twentieth centuries, the very same European nations that had gone through their own struggle for fundamental and human rights dominated entire continents, neatly compartmentalized into colonies, without asking whether the people of the subjugated areas ought to enjoy the same rights.[19] This mixture of freedom and oppression threatened to jeopardize the international communities' effort to internationalize human rights. But all the same, decolonization would have been inconceivable in the latter half of the twentieth century without the simultaneous internationalization of human rights.

Internationalization

During the nineteenth century, progress was made toward the supranational positivization of human rights. Although Kant's idea of cosmopolitan citizenship had conceptually prepared the way, the real impetus came from a literally different field, namely the battlefield of Solferino in 1859, impressively described by Henry Dunant.[20] The horror of that battle led to the establishment of the International Red Cross and the creation of humanitarian international law for the protection of people in armed conflicts. These followed the Geneva Convention of 1864 and are today regulated by the Geneva Conventions of 1949. The Versailles Peace Treaty of 1919 and its clause for the protection of the working class was the next step. It did not negotiate actual guarantees for human rights, but it did found the International Labor Organization (ILO) and formulated international agreements for measures that protect the workforce.

The most important event, however, was the Universal Declaration of Human Rights on 10 December 1948. In knowledge of the atrocities of the Second World War, in December 1948 at the General Assembly of the United Nations Organization (founded in 1945), the worldwide community of nations agreed that the protection of fundamental rights may no longer be left up to individual countries. International law, which since the Peace of Westphalia in 1648 consisted solely in the regulation of relations between nations, was therefore enhanced to include a crucial category, namely the individual human being as a subject of international concern. From then on, international agreements between nations have guaranteed human rights to all human beings, no matter their citizenship, nor whether they were citizens of any country at all. In two respects this implied an axiomatic extension of human rights, or, seen from the opposite perspective, it meant the involvement of every single human being: For one, this agreement includes resident aliens. Though they may not enjoy all rights constitutionally granted to nationals of a given country, aliens remain entitled to the protection of internationally declared human rights. It became necessary, therefore, to make a distinction between fundamental and human rights. Fundamental (sometimes called "basic") rights are generally those rights that hold for citizens of a particular country, while human rights apply to all. For another, for the people of some countries, internationally protected human rights actually mean an enhancement of their entitlements as nationals. International positivization has proven to be an extremely effective instrument especially in countries where national positivization has been slow or was, because of dictatorship, nonexistent. International positivization reveals once more the tension between normativity and reality that is intrinsic to human rights.

The universal declaration of 1948 was merely the beginning of a long undertaking—a promise that had yet to be kept. Legally binding rights had yet to be codified. The General Assembly defined the rights it endorsed as merely "a common standard of achievement for all peoples and all nations" to be accomplished "by progressive measures, national and international." Here a distinction must be made between the international contract itself, as an instrument, and to what these rights, declared in 1948, actually refer. Historically, the declaration of 1948 was a huge step toward the international positivization of human rights. However, much work remained to elaborate what those rights entail, and it was a long way to the institutionalization of international courts where the individual might present his claims. But the declaration itself was a milestone, and in terms of what those rights, devised as "standards," actually mean, in 1990 Norbert Bobbio wrote that 1948 marked merely "the beginning of a long process, … the end of which we cannot yet even fathom." Bobbio also noted that "the Universal Declaration of Human Rights reflects the historical conscience and fundamental values of humanity in the mid-twentieth century. It is a synthesis of the past and a challenge for the future. But those rights have not been carved in stone for all time."[21]

The venture was long and cumbersome particularly because of the discrepancy in the articulation of rights along the divide between the East and the West created by the Cold War. Even the first act of international positivization showed signs of disparate sets of rights. One set covers individual rights of liberty in terms of the citizen's right to rebel against oppression and governmental meddling, in other words, freedom *from* the state. These are also called negative liberties. Another set concerns rights to political participation, in other words, freedom *within* the state, also called positive rights of participation. A third set, finally, involves rights to participate in society, meant to secure adequate standards of living, in other words, freedom *by* or *with the aid* of the state.[22] The divide between the East and West arose from the different priority assigned to these groups of rights. The West gave more priority to individual rights, while the Eastern Bloc gave priority to social rights. For years this controversy delayed the codifying of the ideals of 1948 into covenants. The debate eventually ended with two agreements: On 16 December 1966 the United Nations General Assembly adopted both the "International Covenant on Economic, Social and Cultural Rights" and the "International Covenant on Civil and Political Rights," which are two separate treaties. They did not become valid until 1976, when they were ratified by thirty-five member states.

Western Europe was way ahead of this development. On 4 November 1950 the Council of Europe, founded in 1949 in Strasbourg, passed the European Convention for the Protection of Human Rights and Fundamental Freedoms (ECHR), which came into force in 1953. Its focus was on civil and political rights as they were later to be phrased, slightly altered, for the UN covenant. What was new about the European convention was that it created a right to individual complaint, although it was at first purely facultative and did not need to be recognized by all signatories. Initially it was not possible for a remonstrator to bring an alleged abuse of guaranteed rights directly to the European Court of Human Rights. One had to first approach the European Commission for Human Rights, an intermediate agency that could then take the case to the European Court. Not until 1998 could the European Court of Human Rights directly accept individual complaints of alleged violations of the convention.

In the European Social Charter of 18 October 1961 the Council of Europe articulated economic, social, and cultural rights. In 1995 the social charter was amended by a procedure for collective complaints. On 7 December 2000 the European Parliament, the Council of Ministers, and the European Commission adopted the Charter of Fundamental Rights of the European Union. It meant a further enhancement of fundamental and human rights in Europe, particularly after the Treaty of Lisbon entered into force in 2009, making it positive law within Europe.

Regional treaties were elaborated for the protection of human rights on other continents, too, but compared to the European procedure for submitting grievances these other treaties fall short. Most important for Latin America is the American Convention on Human Rights of 22 November 1969, modeled after the ECHR. Unfortunately the United States and Canada do not acknowledge it. For Africa the African Charter on Human and Peoples' Rights (also known as the Banjul Charter) was approved on 26 June 1981. In practice, however, special instruments for the protection of certain rights, such as the 1969 International Convention on the Elimination of all Forms of Racial Discrimination (ICERD) and the 1987 United Nations Convention against Torture and Other Cruel, Inhuman or Degrading Treatment or Punishment have been more effective than regional treaties. Treaties also exist to guard against the discrimination of women and to protect children's rights and the rights of migrant workers and members of their families.

As mentioned above, to be adequate, any view of the internationalization of human rights must also include the disbanding of colonies from their respective empires. On the one hand, European colonial powers came forward to support the worldwide international positivization of human rights, but on the other hand, they first used force to defend their colonial interests.[23] In 1950 France and Great Britain insisted that their colonial subjects not be covered by the guarantee for human rights stated by the European convention. Instead, they wanted each respective mother country to make special declarations. But as an increasing number of former colonies became independent nations and members of the United Nations, in the early 1960s so-called "Third World" countries constituted the majority there. Both the West and the East tried to influence these young nations, emphasizing their own versions of standards for human rights. To these were soon added a third version, namely postcolonial standards for human rights. In 1960, postcolonial countries drafted the General Assembly's Resolution 1514, the "Declaration on the granting of independence to colonial countries and peoples," eventually achieving the adoption of the right to national self-determination at the UN with the support of the Soviet Union but not that of the West.[24] This right found its way into the United Nations Covenant on Human Rights in 1966 as "the right of peoples to self-determination." Besides the tension between the East and West it was also this process of decolonization following World War Two that made the issue of human rights become a facet of international policy.

The Cold War notably influenced the development of human rights. When the Universal Declaration of Human Rights was adopted in 1948, the Soviet Union and seven other states abstained.[25] The Soviet Union also tried to prevent any publication of the text at home. But within ten years the country's position on foreign affairs changed, and it began to campaign for human rights with a different slant, arguing that without economic, social, and cultural rights, civic and political rights lose meaning. This East-West controversy prolonged efforts at defining the instrument of human rights at the United Nations. But instead of stifling discourse on human rights, the Cold War furthered it. In diplomacy and foreign affairs negotiations continued over just what those rights imply. These were further enhanced by the discussion of postcolonial issues. One aspect that got little attention was the special situation of Europe in contrast to the rest of the world. Driven by an effort to establish human rights in Europe, the initial, past-oriented motivation of "Never again!" was soon supplemented by a will to make a West European mark on the Cold War—one that would also ward off Communism. Thus in the West European context the promotion of human rights itself became a component of the Cold War, thereby feeding into the conflict. It is incorrect to say that the Cold War brought the development of human rights to a halt.[26]

Notes

1. Regina Kreide, *Globale Politik und Menschenrechte. Macht und Ohnmacht eines politischen Instruments* (Frankfurt am Main, 2008), 17ff. This book contains a short survey of numerous theories in support of moral rights.
2. Grimm, "Europäisches Naturrecht und Amerikanische Revolution," 120–51, esp. 120.
3. Wesel, *Geschichte des Rechts in Europa*, 407, 413.
4. Hasso Hofmann calls it a double paradox: On the one hand, the universal claim to autonomy can only be achieved at the level of a particular nation-state. On the other, an individual claim to the right of autonomy can only be achieved in a communal act. See Hofmann, "Menschenrechtliche Autonomieansprüche," 165–73, esp. 165 and 171f.
5. Hasso Hofmann, "Grundrechte 1789—1949—1989," *Neue Juristische Wochenschrift* (1989): 3177–87, esp. 3182.

6. Louis Henkin, "Revolutionen und Verfassungen," in *Zum Begriff der Verfassung*, ed. Ulrich K. Preuss (Frankfurt am Main, 1994), 213–47, esp. 216.
7. Walter Kälin and Jörg Künzli, *Universeller Menschenrechtsschutz* (Basel, Geneva, Munich, 2005), 6.
8. Henkin, "Revolutionen und Verfassungen," 233. See also Hartmut Maurer, "Idee und Wirklichkeit der Grundrechte," *Juristen Zeitung* 14 (1999): 689–97, esp. 690.
9. Wesel, *Geschichte des Rechts in Europa*, 321ff.
10. Hofmann, "Grundrechte 1789—1949—1989," 3179.
11. Wesel, *Geschichte des Rechtes in Europa*, 445ff.
12. Stefan-Ludwig Hoffmann, ed., *Moralpolitik. Geschichte der Menschenrechte im 20. Jahrhundert* (Göttingen, 2010), 16.
13. Hoffmann, *Moralpolitik*, 20f.
14. See Maurer, "Idee und Wirklichkeit der Grundrechte," 689–97, esp. 690f.
15. Hofmann, "Grundrechte 1789—1949—1989," 3179.
16. Horst Dreier, "Grundrechte," in *Grundgesetz Kommentar*, vol. I, Preamble, Article 1–19 (Tübingen, 2004), 55.
17. Erhard Denninger, "Über das Verhältnis von Menschenrechten zum positiven Recht," in *Der gebändigte Leviathan*, ed. E. Denninger (Baden-Baden, 1990), 231–47, esp. 236. See also Möllers, *Das Grundgesetz*, 30ff.
18. Wesel, *Geschichte des Rechts in Europa*, 567, 573ff.
19. Andreas Eckert, "Afrikanische Nationalisten und die Frage der Menschenrechte von den 1940er bis zu den 1970er Jahren," in Hoffmann, *Moralpolitik*, 312–36, esp. 312f.
20. See Kälin and Künzli, *Universeller Menschenrechtsschutz*, 8ff., 15ff., 46ff.
21. Norberto Bobbio, *Das Zeitalter der Menschenrechte. Ist Toleranz durchsetzbar?* (Berlin, 1998), 13, 18. See also Georg Lohmann, "Zur moralischen, juridischen und politischen Dimension der Menschenrechte," in Sandkühler, *Recht und Moral*, 135–50, esp. 149.
22. Bobbio, *Das Zeitalter der Menschenrechte*, 16. A different way of organizing these rights is: positive and negative rights, social rights, and "rights of solidarity among peoples." However, since the third set covers collective rights of protection and self-determination, it cannot be considered as being on the same level as individual rights. See Georg Lohmann, "Die Menschenrechte: unteilbar und gleichgewichtig," in *Die Menschenrechte: unteilbar und gleichgewichtig*, eds. Georg Lohmann, Stefan Gosepath, et al. (Potsdam, 2005), 9. This does not mean that the third set of rights needs no attention. See also Kälin and Künzli, *Universeller Menschenrechtsschutz*, 38.
23. See Fabian Klose, "Menschenrechte, der koloniale Ausnahmezustand und die Radikalisierung der Gewalt," in Hoffmann, *Moralpolitik*, 256–84.
24. Hoffmann, *Moralpolitik*, 26ff.
25. See Jennifer Amos, "Unterstützen und Unterlaufen. Die Sowjetunion und die Allgemeine Erklärung der Menschenrechte, 1948–1958," in Hoffmann, *Moralpolitik*, 142–68.
26. See Mikael Rask Madsen, "Legal Diplomacy. Die europäische Menschenrechtskonvention und der Kalte Krieg," in Hoffmann, *Moralpolitik*, 169–95, esp. 194.

Chapter 5

Human Rights, the State, and Democracy

The national codification of human rights, which were originally considered universal, made those rights part of the positive law of separate nations. In other words, human rights became civil liberties and fundamental rights. That changed human rights from being a question of the philosophy of law to becoming a question of political philosophy. Later, when human rights were codified internationally, that in turn did not change how human rights are related to nationality; it merely redefined the role of the state with respect to human rights. Once human rights became positive law, the chief violator of those rights came to be seen as the state itself. And yet, nationally codifying human rights makes the state the very guarantor of those rights: precautions must be taken to ensure that neither the state itself, nor private agents subject to its laws, violate human rights. Today states are also compelled to negotiate international instruments that protect human rights and safeguard them within their own domestic borders. This has been followed by a willingness of some countries to permit the international investigation of human rights in their country, including the inspection of complaint procedures.

The Role of the State

The codification of human rights proceeded in different countries under widely dissimilar circumstances over a period of two hundred years. The actual process of positivization therefore took on different forms in different places. Even the late eighteenth-century beginnings were different. As we have seen, from the start, the question of what the state and what democracy have to do with human rights was addressed differently in the three countries that initially played the most important role in the development of human rights. Especially how human rights relate to democracy was seen from different standpoints and then went different ways. Although the movements did influence one another—especially between the United States and France (being a matter particularly of personal involvement)—the difference in historical circumstances ultimately led to a difference in how human rights came to be perceived and handled, and this has remained the case to this day.

How Positivization Began in France, the United States, and the United Kingdom

Until the late 1760s, American colonists based their claims against England on their *birthrights as Englishmen*, without mention of independence. Claiming their "natural rights" meant claiming rights as defined by charters of liberties such as the Magna Carta of 1215 or the Bill of Rights of 1689. The introduction to the Bill of Rights of 1689 lists royal offences against traditional order, particularly the monarchy's usurpation of privileges awarded the Parliament, courts, and the church. The American colonists modeled their claims after these older documents, guided conceptually by their English forefathers who "in glorious struggles defended the old liberties against infringement by tyrannical government, and restored them."[1] Just like the English Bill of Rights, Thomas Jefferson's draft for the American Declaration of Independence contained a long list of the English monarch's misdeeds, a detailed record of transgressions.[2] This would have made little sense if the founding fathers had justified national independence using arguments taken from natural law. Instead, the list intended to establish grounds for terminating the allegiance that a king can reasonably expect of his subjects, a royal privilege upheld in Europe from the Middle Ages onward and that followed from how society was organized then. Jefferson's list meant to prove that not the colonists, but the monarch was at fault for the deterioration of the relationship between the sovereign and his subjects: he had failed to protect them. Not until 1774, two years prior to declaring independence, when making their claim not only to their birthrights as Englishmen but also to rights based on the laws of nature, did the colonists introduce ideas from natural law to defend the break from the old country.[3] Even then they called for the restoration of traditional order, in other words, they claimed the right to resist oppression that was given by natural law. This was still in line with classical natural law.

The colonists established their stance using arguments that had originated during a period that for both Continental Europe and England was a thing of the past. That they did so can be explained historically. The first colonists left England in the seventeenth century at a time when debate raged there over these very issues. Ultimately the question was whether the state is bound to a superior right or whether legislation is sovereign. In Continental Europe, Jean Bodin had developed the theory that lawmaking was the task of the sovereign, the absolute ruler. This replaced the medieval notion that divine right (the king's privileged access to God's will) is higher than the state. With the transition from traditional to modern natural law, the king's knowledge of God's will was replaced by human categories of reason. Following the Copernican Revolution in thought on law, effective law was no longer considered just by necessity: right and law did not by necessity coincide. Modern natural law and positive law were no longer one and the same; ideals from modern natural law were used to question the justness of effective law. Natural law became the scholar's tool for questioning absolutist law. In absolutist-ruled France the situation eventually led to revolution, which had far-reaching consequences for human rights.

In England, the idea that there exists a kind of right that is more authoritative than the state remained in place longer. Absolutism there did not have the same thrust that it had on the Continent: British absolutism was restrained by Parliament wrestling compromises from the Crown through various charters of liberties. In these struggles that peaked in the seventeenth century, "sovereignty and the inviolability of rights" became an important argument for clarifying whether some superior, eternal right is greater than both the parliament and the monarch.[4] In the Glorious Revolution of 1688, Parliament had definitely asserted itself against the trend to absolutist monarchy. In theory, the sovereignty of right was victorious, but short-lived. In practice, Parliament soon began disregarding that higher authority. The concept of the unconditional sovereignty of parliament (also known as "parliamentary absolutism") became evermore manifest.[5] Thus, in effect, in England sovereignty of the state replaced sovereignty of right. In France the sovereignty of right had already been replaced by sovereignty of the monarch; in England it was replaced by sovereignty of the parliament. The English Parliament, resting ultimately on the Magna Carta of 1215, was a parliament of classes—organized as the House of Commons and the House of Lords (that included noblemen and the clergy) and the king, who still had his say in lawmaking. The Bill of Rights paved the way for a parliamentary constitution, formally anchoring the sovereignty of Parliament, in 1716. The monarchy was put on new footing in an "alliance of the king and the people" that came to be known as the "king in Parliament." For centuries and to this day in Great Britain the notion of individual liberty is bound to the notion of being represented in this parliament, despite the fact that for a long time only the wealthy had the right to vote.[6]

In the late eighteenth-century conflict with the colonies, England and its parliament were confronted with the old notion of sovereignty of right. The colonists had taken it with them from England a century before and upheld it in the New World. Finding itself in a war-driven need of finances, the English Parliament decided to raise taxes on certain products in America. The colonists refused to accept this measure and confronted England's Parliament with the superior right (an understanding of what is just, morally good or proper) that they had inherited from their English forebears. It was the same superior right that the Parliament had brought against its own monarch one hundred years earlier.[7] "In America the medieval primacy of right remained a reality, although on the Continent and eventually in England, too, it had meanwhile faded into a mere abstract construct of natural law."[8] The colonists watched the laws that they passed in their own local parliaments get examined in London to see whether they conformed to English law. If they did not, they were simply annulled. But more important, the colonists had never been confronted with absolutist claims to rule and had left the struggle with the English Crown up to Parliament far away, in the old country. The colonists stuck to the sovereignty of right. Nothing prompted them, as had happened in England and France, to move toward a sovereignty of the state. "If one had asked Americans of 1776 how natural rights or human rights found their way into positive law, they would have said that they did not find their way into it at all, they had always already been intrinsic to it."[9]

The real circumstances in the colonies helped shape the US understanding of natural law. Once it was evident that traditional order could not be restored and that their birthrights as Englishmen would get them nowhere, the colonists opted for independence; this left them with no traditional English sources for justifying law, and all that remained was to take recourse to natural law. The colonists looked to Locke for theoretical support and took him very pragmatically. Although Locke's *Second Treatise* dealt with England's post-revolutionary government, describing new political institutions in an attempt to give them "greater justification," his theories were nonetheless of a rather general and normative nature[10] and were meant to explain the *ideal* relationship between the individual and the state. In their search for practical solutions, the United States founding fathers interpreted Locke's theory as if the "state of nature" was the very real situation in which they found themselves.

This shaped the US way of thinking about the social contract. For Locke the social contract is a theoretical construct, an imaginary contract among the members of society that only hypothetically precedes the establishment of a state. It is not real.[11] The colonists, however, immediately equated the social contract with the many existing contracts negotiated during the founding of the various states. In doing so, they more or less transformed Locke's social contract into a charter of liberties.[12] Because of their own situation, the colonists understandably thought that Locke's "state of nature," which exists antecedent to men's uniting to create a state, was what they were dealing with. Traversing the continent, settling from east to west, cultivating wilderness far from civilization—this all understandably let them believe that they themselves lived in that "state of nature" discussed in theory. The great difference between their understanding of natural law and that of the Europeans was that the power of the state that the colonists resisted was far away in England. Once it had been shaken off, there was no overpowering state to rebel against. This reduced the tension between natural law and reality: the two converged increasingly until they became one. Thus in North America the conversion of natural law into positive law practically meant simply "renaming" it, while for the French that same conversion meant revolution.[13]

The State as Both Perpetrator and Guarantor of Human Rights

No one has ever doubted that the state can violate human rights. The historical development of the concept of human rights follows precisely from the knowledge that it can. However, in the late eighteenth century, broad consensus arose that the state must somehow also act as guarantor of human rights, even if only by codifying them in individual countries. Thus the state came to be seen as having two roles: that of guaranteeing and that of "naturally opposing" human rights.[14] But above and beyond codifying human rights, what role does the state have in guaranteeing them? Different countries have found quite different answers.

One solution stems from English *common law* and existed long before the positivization of human rights became a topic. Medieval English courts developed a type of jurisprudence based on judicial decisions made for individual cases, also known as precedent. It involved largely the personal liberty of the property owner, protecting him from the grip of the state and from other private persons. Common law did not apply predefined statutes but instead utilized "a spontaneous collection of court decisions accrued by judicial authorities observing one another."[15] Separate from this, Parliament also passed constitutional decrees, the charters of liberties that guaranteed certain civil liberties, for instance the Magna Carta, Petition of Right, the Habeas Corpus Act, and the Bill of Rights. These documents themselves do not make up a constitution; their function was solely to document "inherited" rights and privileges. Great Britain never had a written constitution and remains unique in this respect. Hereditary rights, however, should not be mistaken for human rights; they protected exclusively the political elite, and their purpose was to make the Crown eliminate perceived wrongs.[16]

Since Great Britain's Parliament can only exercise sovereignty by enacting law, the *rule of law* (the maxim that no person is above the law) is of central importance. But that same principle also covers substantial individual freedom that the courts, following common law, must safeguard from abuse by the state.[17] Although the rule of law originally stems from the notion of natural right, while lawmaking in parliament, in contrast, is based on its own sovereignty, in Great Britain the two traditions were never found to be inconsistent. Sovereignty of parliament and the rule of law complement one another. However, the ultimate assertion of the sovereignty of parliament means that no other authority could question it.[18] In other words, the sovereignty of parliament means that the highest guarantee of human rights is a task for the parliament. And yet, because common law exists alongside this sovereignty of parliament, courts at all levels are still crucial to guaranteeing those rights.[19] Because it has no constitution, Great Britain has never had a list of basic rights: "everything was permitted that Parliament had not prohibited."[20] Parliament has the last word, to this day.

Historically speaking, the founding fathers of the United States were the next to deal with the role of the state in safeguarding human rights. The colonists had brought common law across the Atlantic and continued to use it, even after renouncing English rule. The American interpretation of natural rights remained in effect. In it the "state of nature" and natural rights continue to exist, even after a society has set up a political system of government for itself. The *state* and *society* are seen as two different things, and it is the task of government to protect society from developments that might impair its functioning based on the principles of the "state of nature." Originally, the United States needed no bill of rights because even after the establishment of government, individuals retained the natural rights they had before.[21] The rights of individuals are secured by the government: one does not surrender or lose one's rights by establishing government. Unlike for Rousseau, those rights do not become part of political order; it is not necessary to democratically debate or enactment them. For the US founding fathers and for Americans to this day, the power of the state is seen as a threat to natural individual liberty.

Originally, the power of the state meant the same as "government." It was considered sufficient to set up a government that could be dismissed at will and whose main task was to organize the military, the police, and the courts.[22] The founding fathers also worried that the people themselves and their representatives might devise law that violates or hampers individual freedom. The colonists had suffered under the sovereignty of the majority in English Parliament enough to want to curb any such power. To prevent homogenous political majorities they decentralized and dispersed power as much as possible, which eventually led to a fragmentation of the political process. They sought to organize the state without a sole sovereign instance of power and sole utmost authority.[23] But even that was not enough. To safeguard freedom from the populace itself, they created the Supreme Court, the highest court of the United States, to overrule any law passed by the houses and the president, if that law be inconsistent with the provisions of the Constitution.[24] This made the court the final guarantor of natural rights.

The next country to deal with the role of the state as guarantor of human rights was France. There the transition had been made from traditional to modern natural law; natural law had become revolutionary. The struggle was not over reestablishing previous order, and human rights had to conform to the new structures of the state. Freedom was not simply protected by the state, but also created by it; freedom "[did] not arise in the absence of state, by creating pregovernmental or nongoverned spheres, but by the very fact of being democratically constituted."[25] In contrast to the United States, France never fully separated state from society, and one single constitution had to accommodate both. Society, with all its private, commercial, social, and cultural activity, was not considered threatened by statehood: the French Constitution gave society a framework within which it might freely evolve. In line with Rousseau's ideas of the sovereignty of the people, for the French the privilege of liberty could only exist as a formal choice, by law passed by those entitled to it in a voluntary act of equal self-determination. When it depends on the will of the entitled to decide what their rights are, how far these rights extend, and where they end, rights can be established only by the sovereign legislators themselves. This leaves no room for scrutiny of those rights by the courts. In other words, the legislative body remains the guarantor of human rights.

This reveals an aspect in the development of human rights that—despite their differences—France and Great Britain share and that distinguishes them both from the development of human rights in the United States. The concern of these two European nations was to erect legal barriers that would prevent monarchial abuse. We find this expressed in both England's Bill of Rights of 1689 and France's Declaration of the Rights of Man and of the Citizen of 1789. Although these documents were issued in different centuries and followed from different political circumstances, both gave their country's parliaments important functions in this respect.[26] The historical facts behind the transatlantic difference are inarguable: After Hobbes, England made a transition from traditional to modern natural right. After Bodin, France did the same.[27] The United States alone continued to uphold the traditional view of natural right.[28] It would have been inconceivable for England and France to assign the function of the final guarantor of human rights to a supreme court. But in the United States that is exactly what happened, and it was done for historically understandable reasons.

However, the United States and France do share a different tradition that distinguishes them from England. In England the privileges of liberty stem from old class privileges and birthrights that gradually were extended to cover ever-wider circles until they finally became generalized to include all. The United States retained the idea of birthrights but in a qualitative leap turned them into individual rights by giving them a universalistic justification drawn from natural right.[29] France made the same leap by declaring the rights of man and citizens that ultimately do not rest on a declaration of will, but on absolute truth found in natural law. Thus France and the United States have in common the principle of basing the legitimacy of power solely on natural human rights. But that same principle issued different results in these two countries, because each embarked from entirely different historical grounds.

This reveals a different development that was shared by the United States and Great Britain but that separates these two countries from France. The French Revolution was marked by disruptions that were avoided in both England and America. Both England's Glorious Revolution and the American Revolution began "a century-long phase of continuous evolution," while the French Revolution exhibited radical escalation and reactions that led to repeated upheaval.[30] The particular historical backgrounds of the United States and France were each much stronger than their common move toward human rights. In the United States societal change was not only unwelcome, it was deliberately prevented.[31] In France, in contrast, declaring the rights of men and citizens sparked a movement that led "not only to constitutional overthrow, but also to an upheaval in society, and to a revolution in thought, too."[32] Today we see that the treatment of human rights has been durably shaped by this difference. It will become obvious in Part 3, when we return to look at what has happened since the end of the Cold War.

Democratic Legitimacy for Human Rights

The French Revolution changed the principle behind human rights. In a potentially explosive combination, the French bound the idea of freedom guaranteed by natural law to the idea of democracy, leaving the matter precarious ever since.[33] The major breakthrough came when they made personal self-determination a political issue. Individual freedom became interwoven with shared freedom such that individuals granted each other individual liberty through the joint exercising of shared liberty. In other words, personal self-determination is possible when those who are individually entitled to it practice collective self-determination, thereby guaranteeing one another personal freedom. Autonomy thus has both a personal dimension and a collective dimension. Individual and collective autonomy presuppose one another. Without collective autonomy there is no guarantee of personal autonomy, because individuals have no way of obligating one another to respect each other's autonomy. But conversely, collective autonomy must stem from individual autonomy; individuals bring their ideas of personal freedom to the process of lawmaking, which they can do only if they have personal autonomy. Thus individual and collective autonomy dovetail, each being dependent on the other.[34] They are interwoven by legislature, and that makes equality crucial. Citizens that allow one another personal freedom assume that all have the same right to participate in the lawmaking process, in both public discourse and through representatives in legislative bodies. This gives human rights their democratic legitimacy. It hinges freedom with equality.

This process was enabled by the notion of the "nation." Over the centuries, the term "nation" has meant various things.[35] The French Revolution seized the term and declared the nation the locus of sovereignty. The people are sovereign: the people pass law via their representatives in the National Assembly or in Parliament. Together, equally entitled citizens constitute a nation. When the French Revolution began, "nation" meant "the people," without any ethnic connotation whatsoever.[36] The French Constitution of 1793 granted active civil rights to "every foreigner who has reached the age of twenty-one, has lived in France for one year and lives from his earnings or has acquired property or is married to a Frenchwoman, or adopts a child or provides for an elderly person."[37] The French notion of the nation is that of a nation of citizens, but it also involves the idea of universalism. Through naturalization one can become a national, no matter where one comes from. France shares this with the United States. Of course, in reality there was one limitation: even the French Constitution of 1793 did not count women as citizens.

In terms of human rights, in France, sovereignty by the people was then taken to mean that those who are entitled to rights determine those rights themselves. Thus the democratic definition and enactment of human rights meant that they could no longer be deduced from natural right.[38] Although human rights originate in natural right, positivization pries them from that source. Transformation may be slow, initially maintaining the emphasis on natural right and arguing rights from "natural" ideas of human dignity and "human nature," as well as from overall notions of equality that existed prior to positivization and codification. But through positivization those rights are given a genuine definition and often restricted. When claims are then made to these rights or they come to bear in actual cases, their positive legal form becomes increasingly more important and eventually their origins in natural law pale. The only rights that then seem "natural" are those that have not or have not yet been institutionalized. The more often and more accurately human rights are transformed into positive right, both nationally and internationally, the less significant those rights that have not or have not yet been institutionalized but that can still clearly be considered natural rights become.[39]

Democratic legitimation, without which—since the French Revolution—we can no longer imagine grounds for human rights, includes another element that is incompatible with being justified by natural law. Unlike the slow transition described above, the sudden break with tradition at the onset of the revolution, with the Declaration of the Rights of Man and of the Citizens, brought this irreconcilable difference to light.[40] Human rights justified by natural law are prescribed rights. In traditional natural law predetermined right follows from divine right; in modern natural law it follows from human reason. Both forms of natural law assume that only trained experts can properly recognize and assess those rights: it is taken to be a task for scholars. The justification of human rights based on natural law thus means that they will not be openly discussed in political debate. But public debate is open for all, including nonexperts. Human-rights concepts that rest on natural law thus draw the line for democratic discourse this side of those rights. The rights themselves determine the framework within which discourse takes place. That makes it impossible to get democratic legitimacy for those rights. The converse is also true: since these rights themselves outline the framework for democratic procedure, they cannot result from that procedure or be altered by it and cannot be adapted to new events. Human rights established on natural right are oblivious to place and time—they ignore new kinds of suffering and geographically remote suffering, even when these come to our attention. Human rights based on natural law are not malleable per se. They lack the pliability that democratic legitimization could give them.

Majority and Minority

When human rights follow from democratic procedures, the majority defines their content and scope. The results are preceded by debate where representatives express their ideas and seek to achieve a convergence of standpoints, though complete agreement is rare. In constitutional or legislative assemblies, representatives base their positions on discourse from the public arena, all of which is a prerequisite for the democratic legitimization of human rights. When human rights are defined by both public discourse and political assemblies there will always be minorities that are less successful. Making democratically legitimized human rights into law regularly and necessarily ends with some minorities losing out. The dynamic element of the democratic definition of human rights is particularly important for them.

Democratically generated law must always allow for change.[41] Change in law is essential to democracy, because the "sovereign population" changes from year to year: the young come of age and the elderly leave us. This also means that minorities are sometimes only temporary; within the democratic setting they may become majorities. Majorities only exist for certain lengths of time, and minorities likewise. Just prior to the Year of Revolution, 1848, southern German democrat Julius Fröbel said: "By asking members of a minority to surrender their will we are by no means asking them to declare their opinion nonsense, nor are we asking them to give up their cause. We ask only that they suspend it, that they dispense with the practical application of their conviction until they can get more support and the necessary number of people to agree with them."[42] For the democratic legitimization of human rights this still holds. Minorities of opinion can only become majorities if the politically minded public continually rethinks the issues. In consultation that leads to majority decisions, if they want to get consent, representatives must seek solutions that come as close as possible to what is right. Any solution will be imperfect to some extent, because if the outcome is to be positive law and legal stability, at some point a majority decision must terminate the debate. But even then, that termination is not final; majority decisions do not squelch controversy—on the contrary, they may spark new debate. The role of discourse is central to this whole procedure —both broad public debate and political debate among representatives of the people. Fröbel said: "Discussion allows the beliefs of different people to influence one another, it clarifies them, and widens the range of acceptance."[43]

Crucial to the process of debate is the permission to change one's mind. Here the French Revolution's distinction between "*citoyen*" and "*bourgeois*" becomes important.[44] It involves the two roles—the role of coauthoring law and of being subject to the law—in one and the same person. The bourgeois is a citizen pursuing his own personal economic or commercial business. He existed prior to the revolution, although France's feudal system made things more difficult for him than was the case for his partners in commerce in England and America. The revolution placed the *citoyen* at the side of the bourgeois. The *citoyen* brings his own personal experience to political debate, experience that in part also represents his interests as a member of the bourgeoisie. But democratic discussion is a debate among people and their representatives in their function as *citoyens*, not as members of the bourgeoisie. As a *citoyen*, and when confronted with the views and experience of other *citoyens*, the individual must always also reexamine his own position and, if necessary, alter it.

A decision reached by a majority, once participants have discussed an issue and had time and opportunity to convince one another, can be quite different from the decision that would have been reached had there been no interplay of opinions. Imagine an assembly of people seeking to define rules for living together and limiting themselves strictly to their bourgeois interests. The outcome might be the sum of all private interests of all involved. The difference to a political assembly where all parties act as *citoyens* would be that the outcome there not only *would* surpass the sum of all those private interests, but that it *must* extend beyond them. This is because the *citoyen* must ask whether a proposed law can be *willed* by all parties involved.[45] Kant said this in 1793 with an eye to events of the French Revolution. His short piece *On the Saying: That May Be Right in Theory but Won't Work in Practice* advocates the basic idea of the revolution but tries to make the development of the constitution after 1789 appear nonrevolutionary.[46] For Kant, universal will is not the same as the sum of the private interests of all involved. Every *citoyen* must use the criterion of universal validity to examine whether a proposed law is really in the interest of all subject to it. He must first participate in the political debate where all positions are expressed, before he can put himself in the place of all others and understand their standpoints. It is this process that brings forth general, or *universal interest*, or at least an approximation to universal interest, which extends far beyond the sum of all personal interests. In other words, "We ask more of the republican-minded citizen than that he simply pursue his own interests."[47]

Compared to earlier developments in England and America, the French Revolution and its invention of democratic culture created something entirely novel. One could say that the English and the American revolutions did not really become revolutions until reflected by the French Revolution.[48] In terms of human rights, compared to the United States, the French Revolution reveals a difference in the treatment of majorities and minorities. France uses the majority vote to decide what those rights include, and the dynamics of democratic legitimization allow that with time, minorities may become majorities. The protection of minorities comes with time but also from an opportunity to convince one another of political issues. In contrast, even before the French Revolution, the United States founding fathers had already set up institutions to achieve the exact opposite: the decentralizing of power split operative politics into a myriad of minorities. This was supposed to prevent homogeneous majorities, but it also made the protection of minorities a central issue.[49] And it continued to fragment the political process. In terms of human rights, parliamentary majorities can even be vetoed by the Supreme Court, if laws seem inconsistent with principles of the Constitution. Ultimately, the Constitution of the United States is practically insusceptible to modification. This is also true of the fundamental rights guaranteed by its amendments.[50] For example, in 1982 the introduction of a passage on the equal rights of the sexes was abandoned because it was not approved by a sufficient number of states.

Individual Interests and Common Interest

Institutionally organized the way it is, the US system reveals a fundamental peculiarity in the founding fathers' way of thinking that is perceptible not only in the lack of democratic legitimacy for human rights, but in other issues as well, and that peculiarity still exists in the United States today. This way of thinking leaves little or no room for the concept of *common interest* as something distinct from the interests of individuals and something that may oppose them.[51] US political theory always sees the actions of government as actions shaped by underlying individual interests.[52] Processes of political negotiation that would make the envisioned kind of common interest possible in the first place are simply not the focus of American politics. Englishman Thomas Paine (1737–1809), who passionately endorsed the American Revolution, put it quite radically: in *Rights of Man* he said that every real improvement in living conditions must be guided by the personal interests of all individuals:[53] "Every man wishes to pursue his occupation, and to enjoy the fruits of his labors, and the produce of his property in peace and safety, and with the least possible expense. When these things are accomplished, all the objects for which government ought to be established are answered."[54] This actually describes the bourgeois standpoint during the French Revolution.

Paine begins with fundamental principles intrinsic to human nature, which, following the laws of nature, almost surely deliver societal progress. This happens by letting people pursue "the peaceful arts of agriculture, manufacture, and commerce." In that pursuit "the principles of society and civilization operate in man" just as strongly as "instinct [operates] in animals."[55] These principles are thought to be defined by nature and would still exist even "if the formality of government was abolished. The mutual dependence and reciprocal interest which man has upon man, and all the parts of a civilized community upon each other, create that great chain of connection which holds it together."[56] Government should therefore interfere in private matters as little as possible, in order not to disturb or stifle the workings of the laws of nature and progress.

What is crucial here is that government itself is not seen as being above the people but is supposed to arise directly out of society:[57] "That which is called government, or rather that which we ought to conceive government to be, is no more than some common center, in which all the parts of society unite."[58] Locke thought that the natural limits of government were defined by the rights prescribed by the state of nature, the rights that the people brought with them when forming society. Paine simplified things by omitting the transition: society simply remains in a state of nature.[59] He believed that his solution, focused on the individual's natural rights, is easy: "The simple operation of constructing government on the principles of society and the rights of man [retires] every difficulty, and all the parts are brought into cordial unison."[60]

This idiosyncratic neglect of common interest follows from an extreme separation of state, government, and society. It developed in the New World, undeterred by Rousseau or French theories of revolution.[61] Both Great Britain and France endorse a bond between government and society; a bond that thrived during their respective revolutions and still exists today. People pursue their many activities, live their lives, and provide feedback for the political process. Politics and policy making is clearly a mark of government. It provides the framework for a nation or state and society as a whole, and guarantees freedom for societal activity. In Great Britain today, further impulses for liberties flow from the courts' application of common law. This does not weaken the bond between state and society, but strengthens it. Historically speaking, the severing of state from society with the intention of limiting – as much as possible – the government's involvement in and influence on one's personal life is a specifically American phenomenon and can be traced back to the unique circumstances of the country's origins.

Paine's *Rights of Man* became the "textbook" for those of a republican spirit who with President Thomas Jefferson gained leadership of the United States in 1800.[62] "Laissez faire doctrine," the combination of self-regulating society and minimal government, shaped the country and remained unquestioned until the economic crisis of 1929. In the "New Deal" period that followed, President Franklin D. Roosevelt sought to improve social security for citizens through interventionist lawmaking.[63] The Supreme Court declared some of the New Deal's most important elements unconstitutional. Then Roosevelt's overwhelming election victory in 1936 influenced majorities within the Supreme Court in favor of the New Deal. Initiatives toward rudimentarily becoming a socially oriented nation continued until Lyndon B. Johnson's presidency ended. Johnson had pursued several social reforms under a program called the "Great Society." In 1981 Ronald Reagan halted them.[64] The many complaints addressed to the Supreme Court following the introduction of the health insurance law in 2010 reveal how strongly the principle of laissez faire still grips the American people.

It seems therefore completely logical that America's founding fathers saw no need to define fundamental rights in terms of society's collective interest or to legitimate them democratically. For United States citizens, the Constitution put forth the rights "they [already, in a state of nature] had as individuals." It did not articulate rights for them collectively, "as a people."[65] Working out the interest of all was not mandatory for the articulation of fundamental rights. It reminds us of the sovereignty of rights that the colonists brought over from seventeenth-century England and preserved in America, although in Great Britain it had long ago been replaced by a sovereignty of parliament. In the American model, "neither parliament nor the people" is sovereign; sovereign is "the Constitution alone."[66] Paine's *Rights of Man* was explicit: "The government of a free country, properly speaking, is not in the persons, but in the laws. The enacting of those requires no great expense; and when they are administered, the whole [task] of civil government is performed."[67]

Sovereignty By the People

The concept of sovereignty by the people, so central to the French Revolution, was altered and enhanced over the first twenty years following those events. Once the United States had been founded and given a constitution with a preamble that begins "We the People ..." there was much praise for sovereignty by the people.[68] But unlike in France, in the United States sovereignty by the people was not synonymous with "rule by law." The French model of the division of power binds the other powers of state to the normative quality of the law.[69] The legislative, in its function as representative of the people, binds the executive and the administration through general law. In principle, the French system knows no control exercised by a constitutional court. The US version of sovereignty by the people came to understand the division of powers differently. There it rests on "a reciprocal control of partially sovereign organs of the state that can become independent of the will of the people."[70] A crucial element of this is the examination of laws by the Supreme Court, which ultimately leaves no room for participation by the people. Before the nation was officially declared as such, there had been controversy over which version to instate: unlimited sovereignty of the people or limited government. It was uncertain which notion would prevail, even after the nation was established. In 1803 the Supreme Court independently added the examination of laws to its own duties, and the matter was settled. The disappointing turn of events during the French Revolution, combined with a relatively weak political call for unrestricted sovereignty by the people, made that decision palatable.[71] The Supreme Court had thus cut the United States off from the concept of sovereignty by the people that continued to be understood and further developed in Europe. "In contrast to contemporary England and revolutionary France, and in contrast to later interpretations of the American Revolution, it was not the idea of sovereignty by the people that became the foundation for American constitutionalism, but the notion of limited government."[72]

In the three countries that were the first to give a certain shape to the concept of human rights, the forms of those rights can historically be clearly distinguished from one another. While in France democratic legitimacy was crucial to human rights, being the reason and ground for the revolution, the United States—at the federal level—not only has no way to legitimate those rights, but explicitly excludes that option. In Great Britain, on the other hand, the characteristic component is ultimately the sovereignty of Parliament. At all times Parliament has a say on fundamental rights: it can define and limit them with democratic legitimacy.[73] By applying common law the courts there also safeguard fundamental rights. And British court decisions flow back into parliamentary debate without opposing the democratic legitimacy of those rights.[74]

Until the end of World War Two little note was taken of the difference between the French tradition of democratically legitimizing human rights and the slight variation of it that due to a different historical background existed in England, on the one hand, and on the other hand the tradition that existed in the United States of deliberately denying democratic legitimacy for those rights. The difference went unnoticed, because for 150 years the codification of fundamental rights had basically been a domestic matter for nations. In addition, the idea of human rights had also lost luster: the nineteenth century "was not a good century for human rights."[75] The catastrophes of two world wars in the twentieth century further cemented that situation. And throughout the Cold War there was little reason to investigate or discuss the transatlantic discrepancy in the understanding of human rights.[76]

Notes

1. Otto Vossler, "Die amerikanische Revolutionsideale in ihrem Verhältnis zu den europäischen," *Historische Zeitschrift*, supplement 17 (1929): 16.
2. Erich Angermann, "Ständische Rechtstraditionen in der Amerikanischen Unabhängigkeitserklärung," *Historische Zeitschrift* 200 (1965): 61–91, esp. 75.
3. See Habermas, "Naturrecht und Revolution," 108–49, esp. 98f.
4. Otto Vossler, "Studien zur Erklärung der Menschenrechte," *Historische Zeitschrift* 142 (1930): 516–45, esp. 520.
5. Angermann, "Ständische Rechtstraditionen," 89.
6. Preuss, *Zum Begriff der Verfassung*, 13.
7. Angermann, "Ständische Rechtstraditionen," 84.
8. Vossler, "Studien zur Erklärung der Menschenrechte," 516–45, esp. 523.
9. Ibid., 536.
10. Vossler, "Die amerikanischen Revolutionsideale," 18. See also Grimm, "Europäisches Naturrecht und Amerikanische Revolution," 120–151, esp. 135.
11. Of course, Locke himself did say that a "state of Nature" might still exist somewhere, for instance in a situation "of promises and bargains ... between a Swiss and an Indian, in the woods of America." John Locke, *The Second Treatise of Government* (1689), Book II, Ch. 2, § 14.
12. In Locke's theory the social contract is followed by an act of appointing a government, but this is not done with a charter of rule, it is done in an act of "trust." See Euchner, *John Locke*, 33f.
13. Vossler, "Studien zur Erklärung der Menschenrechte," 528f.
14. Klaus Günther, "Rechtspluralismus und universaler Code der Legalität: Globalisierung als rechtstheoretisches Problem," in Günther and Wingert, *Die Öffentliche Vernunft und die Vernunft der Öffentlichkeit*, 539–67, esp. 548.
15. Christoph Möllers, *Die drei Gewalten. Legitimation der Gewaltengliederung in Verfassungsstaat, Europäischer Integration und Internationalisierung* (Weilerswist, 2008), 27.
16. Hofmann, "Zur Herkunft von Menschenrechtserklärungen," 841–48, esp. 845. See also Wesel, *Geschichte des Rechts in Europa*, 315.
17. Möllers, *Die drei Gewalten*, 26.
18. Horst Dippel, "Die Sicherung der Freiheit," 135 –57, esp. 138f. See also Ingeborg Maus, "Verfassung und Verfassungsgebung. Zur Kritik des Theorems einer 'Emergenz' supranationaler und transnationaler Verfassungen," in *Staatliche Souveränität und transnationales Recht*, eds. Regina Kreide and Andreas Niederberger (Mering/Augsburg, 2010), 28–71, esp. 43.
19. Wesel, *Geschichte des Rechts in Europa*, 452.
20. Ibid., 572.
21. Grimm, "Europäisches Naturrecht und Amerikanische Revolution," 120–51, esp. 149. One reason for dispensing with a list of rights in the Constitution was that the division of powers was thought sufficient to secure freedom. See Ingeborg Maus, "Menschenrechte als Ermächtigungsnormen internationaler Politik oder: der zerstörte Zusammenhang von Menschenrechten und Demokratie," in Brunkhorst, Köhler, and Lutz-Bachmann, *Menschenrechte*, 276–92, esp. 283.
22. Grimm, "Europäisches Naturrecht und Amerikanische Revolution," 142.

23. Ibid., 148. See also Ernst Fraenkel, *Das amerikanische Regierungssystem* (Opladen, 1976), 40ff.
24. This authority was not actually stipulated in the Constitution, but the Supreme Court made use of it in a decision in 1803. See Dippel, "Die Sicherung der Freiheit," 135–77, esp. 136.
25. Möllers, *Die Drei Gewalten*, 23.
26. Ibid., 26. Ingeborg Maus suggests that the Constitution of the United States "preserved England's pre-parliamentary system." Maus, *Zur Aufklärung der Demokratietheorie*, 147.
27. Wesel, *Geschichte des Rechts in Europa*, 313f.
28. Habermas, "Naturrecht und Revolution," 108–49, for England, see 98, for France and the United States, see 97.
29. Hofmann, "Menschenrechtliche Autonomieansprüche," 165–73, esp. 168.
30. Anton Pelinka, "Die französische Revolution als Beginn der modernen Demokratieentwicklung" in *Die Französische Revolution und das Projekt der Moderne*, eds. Helmut Reinalter and Anton Pelinka (Vienna, 2002), 217–21, esp. 220.
31. Hofmann, "Grundrechte 1789—1949—1989," 3177 –87, esp. 3178.
32. Ibid., 3179 (Hofmann's italics).
33. According to Habermas, "The *dialectic between liberalism and radical democracy* … exploded worldwide." Jürgen Habermas, "Ist der Herzschlag der Revolution zum Stilstand gekommen? Volkssouveränität als Verfahren. Ein normativer Begriff der Öffentlichkeit?" in *Die Ideen von 1789 in der deutschen Rezeption*, ed. Forum für Philosophie Bad Homburg (Frankfurt am Main, 1989), 7–36, esp. 16 (Habermas's italics).
34. Jürgen Habermas, "Über den internen Zusammenhang von Rechtsstaat und Demokratie", in Menke and Raimondi, 442-453.
35. Gret Haller, *The Limits of Atlanticism: Perceptions of State, Nation, and Religion in Europe and the United States* (New York, 2007), 91ff.
36. Hauke Brunkhorst, "Paradigmenwechsel im Völkerrecht? Lehren aus Bosnien," in *Frieden durch Recht. Kants Friedensidee und das Problem einer neuen Weltordnung*, eds. Matthias Lutz-Bachmann and James Bohmann (Frankfurt am Main, 1996), 251–71, esp. 263f.
37. Maus, *Zur Aufklärung der Demokratietheorie*, 205. The constitution of 1793 never went into effect and was suspended during the Jacobin reign of terror.
38. Habermas, "Zur Legitimation der Menschenrechte," 386–403, esp. 388. See also Menke and Raimondi, *Die Revolution der Menschenrechte*, 11, 247f.
39. Denninger, "Über das Verhältnis von Menschenrechten zum positiven Recht," 231–47, esp. 239.
40. Habermas, "Ist der Herzschlag der Revolution zum Stilstand gekommen?" 7–36, esp. 11f.
41. Habermas, "Über den internen Zusammenhang von Rechtsstaat und Demokratie," 83–94, esp. 84f.
42. Julius Fröbel, *System der sozialen Politik*, Part Two of *Neue Politik*, 2nd edition (Leipzig, 1850), 108f (Fröbel's italics).
43. Fröbel, *System der sozialen Politik*, 96.
44. German translates both as "Bürger," which causes some confusion for the adjective "bürgerlich"; see Ehrhard Eppler, *Der Politik aufs Maul geschaut. Kleines Wörterbuch zum öffentlichen Sprachgebrauch* (Bonn, 2009), 23ff.

45. Bielefeldt, *Kants Symbolik*, 121.
46. Gerd Irrlitz, *Kant Handbuch*, 424.
47. Habermas, *Faktizität und Geltung*, 329.
48. Habermas, "Ist der Herzschlag der Revolution zum Stilstand gekommen?" 7–36, esp. 10f.
49. Fraenkel, *Das amerikanische Regierungssystem*, 40.
50. See Ingeborg Maus, "Verfassung oder Vertrag. Zur Verrechtlichung globaler Politik" in *Anarchie der kommunikativen Freiheit. Jürgen Habermas und die Theorie der internationalen Politik*, eds. Peter Niesen and Benjamin Herborth (Frankfurt am Main, 2007), 350–382, esp. 363ff. For this reason Dippel says that the Constitution of the United States "drops out as a model for other nations." Unfortunately, he continues, in the United States debate over the Constitution unfairly focuses on the federal constitution, while constitutions of the member states are in fact often altered. This is irrelevant for the present topic, because when looking to the US Constitution as a model, other nations have always referred to the federal constitution and its political value. Horst Dippel, *Amerikanische Verfassung: Der Mythos von den selbstverständlichen Wahrheiten* (Kassel, 2006), 3.
51. Grimm, "Europäisches Naturrecht und Amerikanische Revolution," 141.
52. Möllers, *Die drei Gewalten*, 32.
53. Habermas, "Naturrecht und Revolution," 108–49, esp. 112ff.
54. Thomas Paine, *The Rights of Man* (1792), edited by Mark Philp (Oxford, 2008), 251.
55. Ibid., 222.
56. Ibid., 214.
57. Ibid., 120. See also Jürgen Habermas, "Naturrecht und Revolution" in Christoph Menke and Francesca Raimondi, *Die Revolution der Menschenrechte. Grundlegende Texte zu einem neuen Begriff des Politischen* (Berlin, 2011), 108–149, esp. 113.
58. Paine, *The Rights of Man* (1792), 233.
59. Habermas, "Naturrecht und Revolution," 108–49, esp. 101.
60. Paine, *The Rights of Man* (1792), 218.
61. Ernst Fraenkel, *Das amerikanische Regierungssystem*, 41.
62. Vossler, "Die amerikanischen Revolutionsideale,"170.
63. Grimm, "Europäisches Naturrecht und Amerikanische Revolution," 151. See also Fraenkel, *Das amerikanische Regierungssystem*, 189.
64. Jeremy Rifkin, *The European Dream: How Europe's Vision of the Future Is Quietly Eclipsing the American Dream* (New York, 2005).
65. Grimm, "Europäisches Naturrecht und Amerikanische Revolution," 149.
66. Preuss, *Zum Begriff der Verfassung*, 15. The author does say, however, that this should not be taken too literally. And yet, putting it this way does describe the particular mark of the American tradition.
67. Paine, *The Rights of Man* (1792), 237. Dieter Grimm notes that actually Tocqueville understood the American Revolution much better than Paine. But Tocqueville also said that while the United States has a democratic constitution, it never had a democratic revolution. Grimm, "Europäisches Naturrecht und Amerikanische Revolution," 120–151, esp. 134.
68. Dippel, "Die Sicherung der Freiheit," 135ff.

69. Hasso Hofmann, "Geschichtlichkeit und Universalitätsanspruch des Rechtsstaats," *Juristen* Zeitung 1 (1995): 1–32, esp. 22ff.
70. Maus, *Zur Aufklärung der Demokratietheorie*, 230.
71. Dippel, "Die Sicherung der Freiheit," 153f.
72. Ibid., 157. For the traditions of the division of power in these three countries, see Möllers, *Die drei Gewalten*, 19ff. This also explains the title of Part 2 of this book, "Human Rights from 1789 to 1989." While the Virginia Bill of Rights of 1776 does present the first declaration of human rights, it cannot be seen as the starting point for the topic at hand because of other events in the late eighteenth and early nineteenth century. The starting point for what concerns us here can be seen as the year 1789 and the French Revolution.
73. Henkin, "Revolutionen und Verfassungen," 218f.
74. Möllers, *Die drei Gewalten*, 27.
75. Wesel, *Geschichte des Rechts in Europa*, 445.
76. Some scholarly publications did discuss the differences between the French and the American revolutions, but rarely in terms of democratic legitimacy for human rights. See, for example, Hofmann, "Zur Herkunft von Menschenrechtserklärungen," 841–48.

Chapter 6

POLITICS AND LAW

Politics originally meant the management of pubic affairs in the polis, a city-state of ancient Greece. Every polity, be it a nation, member state of a nation, a community, a national alliance, international organization, or union of nations, needs procedures that build and maintain order. Even countries where former order has deteriorated have some sort of politics at work; often some people take up arms and make a claim to power, install dictatorship and demand recognition from other countries. Politics is the management of public power. There is always public power (though it may be disorganized or imperceptible). Monarchies put power in the hands of the monarch, dictators take it into their own hands, and theocracies leave it to religious leaders. But in democracies power is given to the "*demos*," the people.

Today the term "political" has come to often denote partisan politics alone, as if policy making never genuinely takes the common good into account. The common good gets equated with the sum of all those private interests, as if the sum of all private interests represents things without bias and as they truly are. Clearly, this is wrong. When it mirrors merely the sum of all private interests, policy making loses sight of values and neglects the common good. Politics, meaning the management of public affairs, *is* capable of acting in the general interest. Insinuating that politicians are corrupt and incapable of perceiving the general public good may be a self-fulfilling prophecy.

This is especially true for countries where state and governmental order has broken down: there the common good is regularly neglected in favor of private interests. A nation's institutions reveal it: some simply become ineffective; others erode from within and lose their public, in other words, political, function.

Politics and Law at the National Level

Throughout the Cold War, in many separate countries around the world national politics worked with domestic legislation to define human rights. With a few exceptions, most of the results fall into general categories. Politics must specify human rights; law must see that those rights become effective. Thus policy makers must take the first step and enunciate those rights. In many respects, many basic rights need firm installation through legislature. Formal law, for instance, defines the scope of negative liberties and the citizen's right to political participation. Social rights need legislative underpinning in order to become effective. Their strength depends on the introduction of public institutions of welfare, like social security, that must be grounded in law. Democratically elected parliaments pass these laws. In other words, the introduction and definition of fundamental and human rights are a matter of politics.

In contrast, any claim to rights in an individual case is a legal matter. When arriving at a decision for an individual case, government agencies must take account of fundamental and human rights. Those rights can be brought to bear in procedures at all levels. At the national level, assigning responsibility for human rights to politics or to law also involves the question of equality. Essential rights must be guaranteed for all individuals in the same way. The constitution and the law must use broad formulations that apply to all, regardless of personal status and circumstance. Not until a right comes to be claimed in a specific case do personal status and circumstance make any difference.

When fundamental rights are negotiated and defined politically by those entitled to them and their legislative representatives, all parties involved bring their arguments to the debate: philosophical arguments and arguments from natural law, arguments from personal experience, moral and religious arguments, and so on.[1] Naturally, everyone has real situations and people in mind, but these must be generalized for the sake of argument. The arguments that win will be those that pertain to all individuals in the same way. Through debate these arguments get modified to the point that a majority can consent to them. All arguments must pass—as it were—through the eye of a needle, if they are to become acknowledged and applicable law.[2]

Getting Past the Eye of the Needle

The process I call getting past the eye of a needle relates not only to defining essential rights, it applies equally to shaping constitutions and to democratic legislature in general. It marks the origin of law in political debate, the transition from being a political idea to becoming a law, the move toward codification. Codification enables the neutralization of all sorts of reasons that entered into lawmaking. On their way through the eye of the needle, many reasons—moral, religious, and otherwise—become neutral reasons for the purpose of creating law that applies to all. Eliminating bias promotes generality. Moral and religious reasons are personal and group reasons; they lack generality and at first enter the legislative process representing personal or group interests. Majority decisions that back legal norms that are to become valid for all—norms to which other persons may consent for entirely different reasons—must neutralize the bias of that original input.

Although all democratic lawmaking in general seeks majority approval, it is particularly important for the codifying of fundamental and human rights. The eye-of-the-needle process alone makes the rights of one compatible with the rights of all others. The process of eliminating prejudice from argument enables all those involved to realize that other people not only have different interests, but above all, that they have suffered differently because of, or are affected differently by, a particular issue. When interests, experience, and the extent to which people are affected by a given issue conflict, there will be a struggle to find the proper form for a law. Those involved in the controversy come to better understand the real circumstances of the lives of others.[3] This "process of mutual adaptation" creates a deliberate increase in value, something that can only be brought about by taking into account the views of everyone involved.[4] The insight grows that the human right to freedom is only effective when it applies to all. It is important for the democratic legitimacy that is given to human rights by this very procedure. But the value of the negotiation process lies not merely in the resultant democratic legitimacy for human rights. That democratic legitimacy is in itself a seal of approval that guarantees that the formulation of those rights has passed through the eye of the needle and that to a certain extent the rights of one are compatible with the rights of another.[5]

This demonstrates once more how important it is that human rights remain pliable. Human rights started out as the equal rights of a relatively small group of people. Within that context, the concept of equality itself was relative: it related to a specific place and time. During the French Revolution it became obvious that equal rights do not include everyone: women were excluded from participatory citizenship. The times were not ready for women to be seen as equals, just as in the United States it took a long time for blacks, and worldwide an even longer time for indigenous people, to be seen as equals. This illustrates a pattern that is peculiar to human rights. Though they may initially be claimed by a group of privileged persons, with time ever wider circles of people want the same rights and equal treatment. Human rights open gates and widen the circle of those entitled.[6] Years, decades, even centuries may pass from the first articulation of rights to when they become real in practice. Perseverance is sustained for long stretches by the dialectic that exists between normativity and reality, and that is just as much an element of human rights as its own history.

How much human rights depend on geography is shown by the fact that in the late eighteenth century the positivization of basic rights began at the national level. Initially local constraint was essential for positivization to get under way at all. But the decolonization of the twentieth century increased the general awareness that the previous century's growth in equality for the people of Europe rested on a neglect of equality for the people in colonies. Colonialism secured economic growth for Europe at the cost of the colonies. For European countries that economic growth allowed more hitherto underprivileged people to now participate in economic development and public policy making.[7] But to this day equality still depends on where and when you live; equality is not carved in stone for all time. The twenty-first century will show whether equality also involves worldwide access to natural resources. The developments over time and across the globe theoretically all indicate that there no longer exists one outer circle of privileged people that may extend their liberty at the cost of an inner circle. In practice, however, the shift is more toward an approximation of equality, a process that remains open-ended because as time marches on, new groups find themselves excluded for new reasons.

The tendency of human rights to cover ever more aggrieved parties can also be seen the other way around: more and more people want equality. At a certain point in the shaping of rights this can mean restricting the rights of the privileged in order to promote equality for all.[8] For many countries the resistance to women's suffrage can only be explained by the fear that men will lose their privilege. This is true for many rights. In the worldwide struggle over natural resources we can expect to hear similar arguments. When the discussion of human rights comes to the point where former rights must be capped, it becomes mandatory that negotiations involve not only the aggrieved, but the previously privileged as well. Every new arrangement needs new democratic legitimacy, in every respect. Every extension or rewording of human rights once again needs consensus. Those who have been privileged in the past must enter negotiations with those who have been left out. If not, the underprivileged will remain excluded longer, though they eventually will demand radical change.

This is what late eighteenth-century human rights theorists failed to realize. The then-widespread theory of democracy took for granted that there is only one proper solution to a problem and that democratic deliberations bring us closer to it. That is why Kant thought that fair law could also be decreed by an enlightened prince, if he would only conscientiously perform the thought experiment required for determining universal validity. Kant thought that reason followed from the individual's struggle to act in accordance with moral law.[9] Twentieth-century theories of democracy, especially the discourse theory of law, have added to individual human reason a kind of reason achieved through discourse. This reason follows from debate among people and their joint effort to negotiate solutions. It can only take place in the public political forum. But it is also means that the process of deliberative politics must meet certain requirements and guarantee participatory opportunities for all.[10]

Individual and Democratic Legitimacy

The environment in which basic and human rights are applied in individual cases is a different one: it is the context of legal proceedings, not the context of the legislature. Courts and administrative agencies are not where rights acquire democratic legitimacy: it is not the court's task to legitimize law; it is the court's task to determine the legitimacy of the claims of specific individuals.[11]

When we compare the different ways in which the organs that are active in the legislative process and the organs of law and justice proceed, we see why we must make a distinction between individual and democratic legitimacy. For one, policy makers can, at any time, take the initiative and define or redefine human rights. Courts and administrative agencies do not define rights; they deal only with individual cases and then only when someone comes forward as a plaintiff or claimant. For another, courts deal with past events and criteria that have already been fulfilled, in other words, their work is retroactive. Politics, in contrast, is proactive: it generates a framework for the future. And lastly, courts and administrative agencies finalize what will be considered right. Once all options for pursuing the matter further have been either explored or rejected, the outcome is final. The individual has then ultimately gotten "his right," or part of it, or none of it. The law can only sustain stability by being consistent. In contrast, the forming of political will is always incomplete and pliable.

Though we must distinguish democratic legitimacy from individual legitimacy, the two are related. Legitimacy is the outcome of certain procedures pursued by political and legal institutions and agencies—with all the differences described above. It is the relationship of democratic to individual legitimacy that enables self-determined freedom. This becomes clear when we turn to human rights. Conflict can arise when different individuals make a claim to their rights to freedom based on individual self-determination. If at the time of codification the rights in question have been laid out clearly enough, the result will be a case of applying law to an individual claim. An objective interpretation of those rights will help draw a line that limits the right of one such that another can accept the same limit to his own right. But if the solving of general conflicts between a number of individuals—whether or not they consider themselves a group—leads to a situation where rights must be redefined and boundaries redrawn, then legal institutions and agencies alone can no longer solve the problem. They can always only handle the legitimacy of individual claims, which in these cases does not get them any further.[12]

The new solution calls for democratic legitimization, and this can only be achieved through political institutions and agencies, which in turn presuppose individual self-determination in two respects. First, no individual may be excluded if what we want is a decision borne by all who will later be subject to its outcome. We must include everyone to ensure that the granting of rights is reciprocal. The rights of one must be compatible with the rights of all. Each individual must grant every other the same rights, or conversely, he must respect the limits to his own rights, since such rights must be the same for all. Second, everyone involved must feel free to bring their own convictions to political negotiation or to have them brought to a decision-making organ by a representative.[13] Individual self-determination and collective self-determination—autonomy—presuppose one another, and neither has higher rank.[14]

In summary: We can only achieve democratic legitimacy for fundamental and human rights if we first have constitutional and legislative procedures that allow all entitled to those rights to participate in a free and equal manner or to participate via their democratically elected representatives.[15] These procedures can only be provided by a democratic state. Although Kant could not erect his principles on the idea of a democratic state—opting temporarily for the wise ruler who strives for universal validity for his country's laws—he did take an important step in the history of ideas by taking Rousseau's notion of the *volonté générale* and developing it further. The only innate right that Kant sees, namely the right to freedom, can only become real "insofar as each decides the same thing for all and all for each" through legislature by the state and law that applies to all.[16] Conversely, it is precisely the fact that all individuals subject themselves to a purely formal principle of political and legal order that produces well-defined human rights in the first place.[17] Thus we can say that one has a "right to a state."

The Ambivalence of Internationalization

The internationalization of human rights added a new dimension to the distinction between individual and democratic legitimacy. Until after World War Two, passing bills of human rights was a national matter. In Anglo-American regions, liberties continued to develop, in part within the framework of common law and outside of specific canons of basic rights. Politics in the United Kingdom, with its unrestricted sovereignty of Parliament, was in a position to discuss the form of liberties at any time. It refined the definition of fundamental rights, rights that without practical legislation would be impossible to exercise. Democratic legitimacy for fundamental rights was uncontroversial, at least in countries that had developed that tradition following the example of the French Revolution. The application of those rights in individual cases was decided by courts and administration agencies. With a few exceptions, the two areas of politics and law could be kept apart relatively clearly: politics defined rights, and their application in individual cases was a legal matter.

When human rights went international, the distinction between these two categories was blurred. International agreements on human rights are the result of diplomatic negotiation. Diplomats are instructed by their governments to maintain a certain course, achieve minimum goals, or define possible limits through negotiation. Once an agreement has been reached, documents are signed by the governments that accept the result. These documents do not become valid for any contracting state until they have been ratified by its national parliament. The actual text then becomes inalterable: neither its content nor the specification of the rights to which it pertains is subject to democratic negotiation. However, ratification by a "domestic *demos*" cannot be a substitute for the democratic process of deliberation.[18] Even in cases where a human right defined in international covenants needs practical national legislation in order to become effectual at all,[19] we must not confuse the ratification of those laws with the procedure that leads to legitimizing them democratically. The former has no room for open public debate on the content or specifications of those rights once they have been predefined at the international level.

When international covenants on human rights include the right to complaint by the individual and a court or other instance for complaint has been set up, the same thing happens, in principle, as would happen at the national level. Just as national courts apply basic and human rights in individual cases, or examine their applicability, the courts or instances of complaint that have been set up based on international agreements do the same. Since human rights have become internationalized, the amount of examination done by national courts has risen considerably, because now they must not only see that nationally guaranteed basic rights are protected, but that internationally confirmed rights are protected as well. International law obligates states to set up instances of complaint where grievances related to the violation of international guarantees of human rights can be brought forward at home. In many countries these are regular courts.

We have no internationally elected parliaments that can negotiate human rights or specify what they entail. In Europe some steps have been taken in the right direction, but none of them are responsible for the final say when it comes to basic rights. In Part 4 we shall return to discuss various regional approaches. Currently there exists no international institution that can provide human rights with democratic legitimacy.[20] Under these circumstances, international courts and other agencies inevitably accept complaints of violations of human rights and continue to develop human rights, adjusting them to new needs. Simultaneously, however, this means that true democratic legitimacy is being replaced by individual legitimacy—and this has grave consequences. These consequences become clear when contrasted with the national level. At the national level we can compare—in original size as it were—the features peculiar to procedures used by political organs and organs of law and justice. At the international level we cannot even make that comparison, because there simply are no democratically elected organs whose responsibility it would be to positivize human rights.

But when instead of being taken care of by political bodies, it is left up to the courts to further develop basic and human rights, the development stalls. Courts are confined to fields for which complaints and grievances are submitted at all. And even then rulings tend to become inflexible, because it takes elaborate reasons to rule on a new but similar case differently than was ruled in a previous case. In contrast, when it is up to political organs to further develop basic and human rights, that development always remains open and can better take into account new developments within society. Compared to legislature, court cases always involve a degree of "individualizing." This has consequences for basic and human rights, particularly when the decision involves the conflicting rights of various parties.[21] In cases such as these, rights tend to be formulated not in a general way, but individually, dependent on the particular situation, and that may possibly not be representative of the overall problem for which it is necessary to determine the scope of that right in general. Many elements of court hearings are much more random than those of democratic negotiation. Winning a case can depend on a lawyer's assertiveness and on whether one has the means to initiate and execute proceedings at all.

The main fault of court decisions within the context of democratic legitimization is that they exclude from the process of determining rights all others that are also "beneficiaries." The decision of how to distribute liberties is taken out of the hand of the democratic lawmaker. When, in an individual case, a person is confronted with the government, it is less obvious that he may be dealing with an absence of democratic legitimization. That absence becomes clearly visible, however, when people assert their rights against one another in the same way as private owners assert their property rights. This will not only result in an understanding on the part of those involved in human rights as boiling down to private rights analogous to property rights, but it will also mean that the courts will become a place where rights that clash in an individual case are weighed against each other in such a way as to produce a generalizing effect on comparable cases. In the meantime, it is easily forgotten that the limits to human rights must primarily be drawn by those who themselves possess general and identical human rights—that is, by the subjects of human rights themselves, and not by a court. The concordance between potentially conflicting human rights thus also requires an abstract and general arrangement in which the interests of all the subjects of human rights are taken into account independently of an actual individual case.[22]

The Dilemma and Its Repercussions at the National Level

The internationalization of human rights makes the dilemma inherent to human rights clearer than ever. Making human rights universal fundamentally and inextricably contradicts legitimizing them democratically. Historically speaking, the dilemma became apparent in two phases. The first positivization of human rights occurred at the level of individual nations, particularly within the context of the very creation of those nations. Geographical limitation was a straightforward prerequisite for positivizing rights at all. This was done at the cost of their universality. Although the words chosen to articulate human rights, for instance in the French Declaration of the Rights of Men and of the Citizen, appeal to universality, the fact remains that only the citizens of the declaring nation can claim the rights defined by their own list. The democratic legitimacy of human rights is at odds with their being universal. The exact opposite happened when human rights became internationalized. Those rights then had universal applicability but lost democratic legitimacy. Through internationalization the downside of national codification was partially balanced, as it were, but this, in turn, at the cost of democratic legitimacy. We have no democratically elected institutions at the international level that are authorized to make decisions on human rights; once human rights are universal, it is impossible to democratically legitimize them.[23]

The dilemma of democratically legitimizing universal human rights can only be solved by creating a worldwide democracy with a world parliament that represents the entirety of mankind and decides what human rights are. Obviously it is questionable whether we should aspire to that sort of state. Kant considered it and clearly rejected any such kind of world-state; it would be, he thought, impossible to govern. He preferred a balance of powers that would "gradually bring people nearer to agreement on which principals lead to peace." A world-state, he thought, would end in a "graveyard of freedom."[24] From today's perspective and for the near future, it is highly unlikely that we can create worldwide structures that would allow the direct democratic legitimization of human rights that claim to be universal—and that is good. But knowing that at least for the near future we cannot, at an international level, give human rights the same democratic legitimacy that they can attain at the national level, we must nonetheless dare to initiate an incremental process of assimilation. In Part 4 we shall return to discuss this.

The tension between universality and democratic legitimacy has shaped basic and human rights since their first positivization. Even today it constitutes the framework within which individual nation-states position themselves. The particular history of each state plays an important part in that constellation. As we have seen in comparing the different historical starting points of the first three nations to pursue the positivization of rights, there were already massive differences in the significance each attributed to democratic legitimization. More important is the experience that each country gained through that process. Depending on its own history, each one of these countries saw either the executive, the legislative (at best including the people), or the courts as a threat to freedom. Whether democratic legitimacy is more or less important for liberties has depended on how great that threat was perceived to be.[25]

Of crucial importance, however, is that that past experience not only shapes the attitude that individual nations have toward their own domestic basic rights but that it also informs their view of internationally guaranteed human rights. The opposite is also true: a lack of internationally guaranteed rights can raise esteem for the democratic legitimacy of domestic rights.[26] This is why the paradox of universality and democratic legitimacy prompted a particular development at the national level: even in countries that (based on the French Revolution) have a tradition of achieving democratic legitimacy for domestic basic rights, we can currently observe a tendency toward a loss of esteem for that democratic legitimacy.

Beyond doubt, after the harrowing Second World War, the internationalization of human rights meant a breakthrough that cannot be praised enough. But I must repeat what Norbert Bobbio wrote after the end of the Cold War about the UN Universal Declaration of Human Rights. The year 1948, he wrote, marks the "beginning of a long process … , the end of which we cannot yet even fathom."[27] What we need today is a broad reflection on basic and human rights that also analyzes the intertwining of regional, national, and worldwide aspects. Essentially, the internationalization of human rights has led to the instatement of individual legitimizing in place of democratic legitimization. This means that at the international level, too, the compatibility of the rights of one with the rights of all others can no longer be achieved via the democratic legitimization of rights but will also have to take the route of individual legitimacy for individual cases.

Another consequence of replacing democratic legitimacy with the legitimacy of individual claims is that it robs human rights of a central feature, namely, the inherent tie of freedom to equality. Since there is no negotiating among all beneficiaries, the hinge is lost that otherwise links freedom to equality. The gate-opening function of human rights that lets these rights extend to ever more circles of people will make that loss of the link between freedom and equality a major theme of the twenty-first century. It will be crucial for the discussion of global access to natural resources. The mechanisms that align the rights of the individual with the rights of all others will be important. We shall return to this aspect in Part 4, as well.

Notes

1. For a discussion of religious arguments see Thomas M. Schmidt, "Vernunftrecht und göttliche Gebote. Religion als vorpolitische Quelle der Menschenrechte?" in *Die Freiheit der Religion im europäischen Verfassungsrecht*, eds. Stefan Kadelbach and Barinas Parhisi (Baden-Baden, 2007), 15–27.
2. Within the context of how government and administration is bound to justice and law, Jürgen Habermas's choice of metaphor is that when democratically generating opinion and public will, procedural and communication prerequisites function as a "sluice gate." Jürgen Habermas, *Die Einbeziehung des Anderen. Studien zur politischen Theorie* (Frankfurt am Main, 1996), 289.
3. Schmidt, "Vernunftrecht und göttliche Gebote," 15–27.
4. Klaus Günther, "Liberale und diskurstheoretische Deutung der Menschenrechte," in *Rechtsphilosophie im 21. Jahrhundert*, eds. Winfried Brugger, Ulfrid Neumann, and Stephan Kirste (Frankfurt am Main, 2008), p. 346.
5. Gret Haller, "Individualisierung der Menschenrechte? Die kollektive—demokratische—Dimension der Menschenrechte und ihre Bedeutung für Integrationsprozesse, illustriert durch das Beispiel des State-Building in Bosnien & Herzegowina," *Zeitschrift für Rechtssoziologie* 31 (2010): 129.
6. Günther, "Liberale und diskurstheoretische Deutung der Menschenrechte," 393.
7. Hoffmann, *Moralpolitik*, 16.
8. Menke and Raimondi, *Die Revolution der Menschenrechte*, 9.
9. Heiner Bielefeldt points out that Kant did pursue a communicative approach. See Bielefeldt, *Kants Symbolik*, 23. Ingeborg Maus also notes that Kant recommended a "non-monological" decision process for legislation. See Maus, *Zur Aufklärung der Demokratietheorie*, 330. See also Maus, "Freiheitsrechte und Volkssouveränität," 507–62, esp. 549.
10. Habermas, *Faktizität und Geltung*, 349ff.
11. Möllers, *Die drei Gewalten*, 87ff.
12. Ibid., 73ff.
13. On the importance of absolute individualism for the process of democratically determining the general will, see Brunkhorst, "Paradigmenwechsel im Völkerrecht? Lehren aus Bosnien," 251–71, esp. 265.
14. Habermas, "Zur Legitimation der Menschenrechte," 386–403, esp. 391.
15. Maus, *Zur Aufklärung der Demokratietheorie*, 331ff.
16. Immanuel Kant, *Metaphysik der Sitten* (1797), German Academy Edition vol. VI, 314.
17. Bielefeldt, *Kants Symbolik*, 117f.
18. Peter Niesen, "Deliberation ohne Demokratie? Zur Konstruktion von Legitimität jenseits des Nationalstaates" in *Transnationale Verrechtlichung. Nationale Demokratien im Kontext globaler Politik*, ed. Regina Kreide (Frankfurt and New York, 2008), 240–259, esp. 248.
19. This is the case, for example, with conventions against racism that oblige member states to punish the spread of racist statements.
20. Klaus Günther, "From a Gubernative to a Deliberative Human Rights Policy Definition, and Further Development of Human Rights as an Act of Collective

Self-determination" in *Definition and Development of Human Rights and Popular Sovereignty in Europe*, ed. Council of Europe Publishing (Strasbourg 2011), p. 35–45, esp. 39. See also Christoph Möllers, *Gewaltengliederung. Legitimation und Dogmatik im nationalen und internationalen Rechtsvergleich* (Tübingen, 2005), 156.

21. Möllers, *Die Drei Gewalten*, 144ff.
22. Günther, "From a Gubernative to a Deliberative Human Rights Policy Definition, and Further Development of Human Rights as an Act of Collective Self-determination." Möllers finds the task of distributing liberty one to be defined by legislation—not by law-bound courts—primarily because lawmakers have at their disposal other ways for achieving compromise.
23. See Isabelle Ley, "Kant *versus* Locke: Europarechtlicher und völkerrechtlicher Konstitutionalismus im Vergleich," *Zeitschrift für ausländisches öffentliches Recht und Völkerrecht* 2 (2009): 317–45, esp. 339.
24. Immanuel Kant, *Zum ewigen Frieden* [Perpetual Peace], 1795, German Academy Edition, vol. VIII, 367.
25. Möllers, *Die Drei Gewalten*, 20.
26. Gret Haller, "Introduction," in *Definition and Development of Human Rights and Popular Sovereignty in Europe*, 9–31, esp. p. 22.
27. Bobbio, *Das Zeitalter der Menschenrechte*, 13.

Part III

The Crisis in Human Rights Since 1989

The meaning of human rights has changed since the end of the Cold War. The demise of Communist dictatorship was welcomed with both great relief and hope for a rapid breakthrough in human rights. That aspiration was realized in part by numerous new democracies that integrated canons of human rights into their constitutions, thus enabling the genuine exercise of those guaranteed rights. But at the same time statements began to circulate that should have caused alarm. Political scientist Francis Fukuyama, for instance, remarked that those events marked the "end of history." Looking back over the two decades that have passed since the end of the Cold War we can see a crisis in human rights, a crisis that obviously began at the very moment people were celebrating their newfound freedom. Before examining that crisis, we need to first understand the human rights situation between 1945 and 1989 on both sides of the iron curtain. Some features of that period are of particular importance for the crisis that followed. We will later turn to crucial events after 1989.

Chapter 7

The Cold War

The years following 1945 initially saw a major breakthrough for basic and human rights, when several nations converted those rights into positive domestic law. Great Britain, however, having no constitution and no catalog of basic rights, remained untouched by that development. It had maintained its tradition of continually extending the birthrights of its countrymen. There was no revolution; change took place in small steps that in the early nineteenth century had just barely prevented an armed uprising.[1] What the labor force wanted was to be more adequately represented in Parliament. That practically doubled the number of eligible voters, although taking one thing at a time, the general right to vote for all (male) citizens did not come until later.

In Great Britain the right to resistance, based on natural law, was still in effect, but following a tradition older than the French Revolution, the extension of other rights occurred by extending the active right to vote. Thus in various respects, in Britain the struggle for human rights always went through Parliament. There was a struggle for the equal right to vote for all and a struggle to weaken the influence of the Crown and the Upper House in Parliament that allowed the sovereignty of Parliament to develop toward a sovereignty of the people. And finally, the Parliament itself struggled to enact law that would enable the enforcement of social rights, although these were not defined in any formal canon of basic rights. A British set of basic human rights was not outlined until 1998, when the Human Rights

Act incorporated the European Convention on Human Rights into domestic law—forty-five years after it had first come into effect in 1953. It was sensational for the concept of rights in Britain.[2] The United Kingdom has a unique capacity for introducing innovation incrementally, which is in part due to the long tradition reflected by its institutions. That perseverance is also an expression of never having shied from carefully adapting those institutions to modern circumstances.[3]

The decisive breakthrough in the national positivization of human rights took place in the Federal Republic of Germany, where the greatest effort was undertaken to prevent the new constitution from suffering the same fate as that of the Weimar Constitution, which ended in National Socialism. Besides including the canon of basic rights, the West German Constitution (now valid for reunited Germany) says that certain clauses may not be altered, especially the passages on human dignity, democracy, and the rule of law. The establishment of a strong constitutional court in West Germany enabled successful jurisdiction for fundamental rights. The Federal Constitutional Court was given the authority to cancel laws passed by the German parliament if it sees therein a violation of the laws of the constitution. When it comes to protecting fundamental rights, the current German Constitutional Court has a greater influence on the division of power than the United States Supreme Court.[4]

Looking back, when the Cold War began, the three countries among the first to shape human rights, namely France, the United States, and Great Britain, were joined by a fourth, the Federal Republic of Germany, which significantly influenced the further development of the concept. Important for the question of the democratic legitimacy of basic and human rights is the fact that with this development the scales tipped in favor of the view that in terms of human rights, democratic legitimization is not the utmost concern—a stance that historically came mainly from the United States.

East-West Confrontation

During the Cold War, the topic of human rights received much attention, although the Western and Eastern bloc countries stressed different groups of rights. Alliances in both the East and West used "the language of human rights as a weapon."[5] One controversy concerned the role of the state. The Eastern bloc countries' emphasis on economic, social, and cultural rights called for active government, because it saw one premise of the realization of those rights as being freedom *by way of* or *through* the aid of the state.[6] On the other hand, this also involved disagreement on the relationship between freedom and equality. "No equality without freedom" said the West, and "No freedom without equality" said the East. Each camp defined its own position in light of the other, with increasing acerbity. The more the East stressed equality and the role of the state, the more transparently the West stressed liberty and freedom *from* the state. The West also consistently stressed political rights, in other words, the positive right to participate in governing—freedom *within* the state in contrast to the totalitarian situation in the East. The East's habitual response was to say that without equality, freedom remains an illusion and that the same holds for the right to political participation without the granting of social rights. All the while, the real living conditions of the people behind the iron curtain bitterly contradicted the jargon used by their government in politics and diplomacy. The people suffered not only from a lack of political freedom, but in many regions also from extremely precarious economic circumstances. Only a few of the Soviet Union's satellite states had tolerable economic conditions. But political conditions were no better there, either.

Surprisingly, during this same period in Western Europe, located between the two superpowers and their dispute, social rights got an unprecedented boost. Western Europe clearly saw itself as belonging to the West, even being the West's bridgehead opposite the East. But the proximity to the East influenced European developments. This is elucidated by the unparalleled development of institutions based on the European Convention for Human Rights. The atrocities of the war were the initial mainspring of that development. But soon the East-West confrontation became an equally strong motive.[7] In addition, the nations of Western Europe continued to develop the welfare state, albeit to differing degrees. Coming to terms with its own past was a significant factor for the development of human rights in West Germany. The 1930s economic crisis had horrifically nurtured National Socialism. But Germany had an older tradition to which it could return: at the end of the nineteenth century Bismarck's introduction of social insurance had already institutionalized a European first that some have called "the authorities' prudent response to the social issue."[8] Nonetheless, in Western Europe during the decades following World War Two, the economic boom also encouraged a strengthening of social institutions. And yet, in terms of being a political motivation, the competition between the West and the East should not be underestimated. Throughout the first decades of the Cold War that competition was crucial. As early as 1961, the European Social Charter became a Western European common denominator for social statehood.

As the overall confrontation of the two major blocs took hold, Europe responded to propaganda from the East—propaganda couched in the very language of human rights—by moving on, taking all three sets of rights equally seriously: freedom *from* the state, freedom *within* the state, and freedom *by way of* the state. It was beyond doubt that legislature was needed in order to genuinely realize and practice fundamental and human rights. And the necessary laws were written democratically by parliaments of representatives elected by the citizens. In practice this meant that at the national level the decision as to how far certain rights extended was made democratically. Under these circumstances the democratic legitimacy of fundamental and human rights was rarely an issue. In practice, the organs of the European Convention on Human Rights were rather reserved during the first two decades.[9] In contrast, the West German Constitutional Court quickly broadened its jurisdiction on basic rights by also evaluating violations of basic rights ensuing from actions by third parties.[10]

The Western European trend toward the welfare state was not much different from developments in the United States, where the New Deal still guided the course. But in the United States that was an exceptional situation that only lasted until the late 1970s.

Natural Right and Revolution

In terms of the history of ideas, the roots of the Cold War go back further than a century. For human rights, the first events of significance were those of the late eighteenth century, but later Karl Marx's word became eminent. His work *On the Jewish Question*, written in 1843, was chiefly about freedom of religion but went on to discuss human and citizen rights in general and came to a harsh conclusion. Marx saw the assertion of human rights in America and France as merely supportive of the individual pursuit of private economic interests without social constraint. "So-called human rights," he said, are nothing but "the rights of someone from the bourgeois class, in other words, the rights of the egoistic individual, one isolated from the community and others."[11] Private property, he said, had isolated itself from the community, and in order to protect it, the bourgeoisie had devised the state, an entity outside of and parallel to the community. The state and its laws protect the owners' property for them.[12] The modern state, in other words, serves the sole purpose of protecting property and property owner interests.

Marx's view appears to pick up where Thomas Paine left off. Paine, too, saw society and the state as two distinct entities and the indulgent interests of individuals as the sole motor of development. According to Paine, common interest that extends beyond individual interests is not only superfluous; it is detrimental to social development. That notion gained ground particularly in America.

In fact, Marx wrote with an eye to North America, saying explicitly that the United States was the perfect example of the sort of modern state he questioned. When Marx wrote of revolution, disqualifying it as merely "political" as opposed to "proletarian" revolution, he meant revolution based on natural law, taken from the Anglo-Saxon tradition of natural law that never got past the right to resistance and had no place for revolution the way the French understood it.[13] Marx's description of human rights, based on revolutions of the late eighteenth century, ignores the aspect of equality raised by the French Revolution. He had his own interpretation of the French declaration of rights for "men and citizens." For Marx the revolutions of the late eighteenth century had only liberated the bourgeois citizen legally; the social liberation of "the people" could only be had by a revolution of the proletariat. His assumption (that came to overpower all others) was that the unleashing of private interests deteriorated society as a whole by splitting it up into mere individuals. This view leaves no room for the idea that as citizens, individuals might themselves define human rights such that these include the normative element of equality. Marx was trapped by his own ideological premise; he ignored "those elements of the declaration of human rights that lie beyond the charm of ideology."[14] Nonetheless, it is striking how similar Paine and Marx are in their reducing of the issue to one of the bourgeois, despite the fact that they wrote at different times and in evaluating the events of the late eighteenth century arrived at entirely different conclusions.

On both sides of the Atlantic the revolutionaries had drawn their arguments from natural law. Both the founding fathers of the United States and the revolutionaries of France saw themselves as converting natural law into positive law, albeit in different ways. The United States took a liberal stance on natural right, where natural laws coincide with social principles, as Paine so enthusiastically depicted. Society and the government remain separate entities so that social forces can work without impediment by the government. France, in contrast, took the revolutionary step—based also on Rousseau's philosophical ideas and that of the *volonté générale*—of erecting a fundamentally new order for both the state and society meant to back the productive development of social forces.[15] In the United States events were not considered revolutionary until the year 1800 and the election of Thomas Jefferson as president. Even then, talk was of "the revolution of 1800."[16] As we have seen, the two countries meant different things by "revolution," because they had different traditions of natural law.[17] Despite these differences that were oblivious to the populace, in the early nineteenth century natural law and revolution were considered compatible.

In the nineteenth century the importance of rationalizations drawn from natural law dwindled and positive right came to the fore.[18] In Europe revolutions came to be frowned upon after France ended up with Napoleon and his conquests across the continent. And Marx's theories added a new dimension to the fear of upheavals. The proletarian revolution that Marx wanted was not based on the positivization of natural law that despite all their differences the American and the French revolutions did have in common. Marx severed revolution from rights and made it—as it were—an automatic process of natural history. Striking, once again, is the parallel to Paine, who also believed in natural social processes that were to be left undisturbed by man-made law. Marx went on to discredit law in general by declaring it an instrument of control and influence for the class of property owners. In doing so he disjoined revolution from natural law. The two components that had contributed to the development of freedom and equality, each in its own way, fell apart. As of 1917 and the October Revolution, each had its own locus. The "heritage had been clearly divided in a fateful way: one side put claim to revolution, and the other inherited the ideology of natural rights."[19]

After 1948 the Soviet Union abandoned Marxist doctrine by after having initially dismissed human rights, it then made them one of its own implements for fighting the ideological battles of the Cold War. Nevertheless, the East-West controversy did indirectly reflect the two now-separate parts of the concept, namely natural law and revolution, particularly when it came to the role of the state. At the cost of freedom, the totalitarian state enforced equality, or at least claimed it to be its ideological, and originally revolutionary, intention. From the perspective of the West, such a state needs constraining. The human rights allegedly capable of exerting that constraint were taken to be pregovernmental and justified by natural law. Thus ultimately the Cold War uniquely confirmed the division of the historical legacy. In terms of human rights, the United States, in the role it had as the leader of the West, was confirmed in its classical understanding of natural rights. This was particularly true for the right to oppose totalitarian government, much of which existed in the East. And with the end of the Cold War, the ideology of revolution had definitely been proven wrong.

New Interventionism

Looking back over the years that have passed since the end of the Cold War, we see that the end of that phase actually opened the door for new interventionism, and that it too was done in the name of human rights. The old "balance of fear" had previously apparently deterred some states from trying to authoritatively advance human rights in other states. The key for meddling now came by the name of "humanitarian intervention," which, ironically, was actually of a military nature. Human rights got degraded to a catchphrase that seemed to justify military intervention. Now, it is extremely controversial to justify military intervention by claiming to protect human rights. The initial justification for the second war in Iraq was the need to destroy weapons of mass destruction. That had far-reaching consequences for human rights. Once those grounds proved to be false, the new claim became, once again, the need to protect human rights. It demoted human rights to the status of a mere "hegemonic technique of international politics used by various conflicting parties to give their own particular interests a universal slant."[20]

The circumstances preceding various instances of intervention have varied. In some cases it has been a matter of controversy whether a particular intervention was compatible with international law; for other cases it has been clearly refuted. Exactly which is true cannot be explored here; for our present purpose it is important to look at the understanding of human rights used to back those cases of intervention. The fact that military intervention itself always involves violations of human rights is only part of the problem. Every act of intervention has some idea of what the troubled state should look like afterward. The intervening powers set that idea in motion as soon as military peace has been attained, if not sooner. The role that these plans give human rights is the other part of the problem. All four interventions undertaken during the first twenty years after the end of the Cold War have had one thing in common: the building, or rebuilding, of the nations in question was based on one and the same model, namely, a model that established order on the basis of belonging to ethnic or religious groups.

For several reasons the intervention in Bosnia and Herzegovina has a special place in this series. It began in 1995 and thus heads the list of regions where the reconstruction of state was based on ethnic or religious organization. In Bosnia a model of state-building was used that came to be employed in Kosovo, Afghanistan, and then Iraq. In contrast to subsequent interventions, the intervention in Bosnia was clearly backed by international law and was undertaken by NATO based on a resolution passed by the United Nations Security Council. Military pacification was achieved within months. Of course, that intervention occurred relatively late during the overall conflict, happening four years after the war was already under way in Bosnia and many had been killed. When the international community went about rebuilding state institutions, the issue of human rights played a major role. Compared to all nonmilitary effort invested, the part of reconstruction devoted to human rights was much greater than in any other region of crisis later to become the target of intervention. The relatively fast achievement of military pacification in Bosnia allows a better evaluation of the human rights–related activity there than for the other three regions of later intervention. While for the other three critical regions the challenges of military pacification were always predominant, a fact that heavily restricted efforts at improving human rights, for Bosnia it is fairly clear how rebuilding the state influenced the human rights situation, independent of military events. It makes Bosnia especially important for how human rights came to be understood in post–Cold War times.

Bosnia and Herzegovina

The reconstruction of state that followed the war in Bosnia was based entirely on the Dayton peace agreement, designed for the most part by the United States administration. In that accord, human rights were awarded a central role characterized by three features.[21] The first was the pattern described above, where public order is established on ethnicity. The fact that military demarcation lines more or less became new territorial boundaries within the federation can be explained by how the agreement came about: negotiations in Dayton included the warlords. But even beyond the definition of those borders, the relevance of ethnicity was pursued right down to the finest federalist structures of the country in a way that had never before existed in centuries of Bosnian history. For one, the Dayton accord split the presidency into three parts, each one of which represents one of the three major ethnic groups of Bosnian Serbs, Bosnian Croats, and Bosniaks.[22] For another, through the Dayton accord the international community forced a constitution on the new nation. In addition, the accord declared all worldwide and European conventions for the protection of human rights to be immediately applicable in Bosnia. Then a large number of complaint options were created at various administrative levels, both national and regional, to which individuals could resort, where one could bring forward violations of basic and human rights guaranteed by the peace agreement.

The international community came to see the Dayton Agreement as inviolable; the people of Bosnia at first even regarded it as sacrosanct. The international parties involved made every effort to tamp down discussion of the actual contents of the accord. Theoretically, one can understand the desire to ignore protest against a legal document devised to restore stability after four years of war, ethnic expulsion, and massive war crimes. But in practice, and in combination with the features described above, the refusal to question the contents of the agreement contributed to delaying social peace for a long time. One example: In 1996, immediately after the war ended, people began claiming that their human rights had been violated *because* they belonged to a certain ethnic group. Victims argued that their rights "*as* Bosnian Croats," "*as* Bosnian Serbs," or "*as* Bosniaks" had been violated. These arguments were often linked explicitly or implicitly to the notion that the members of the ethnic group to which the offenders belonged had lost their right to human rights. Their deeds were so atrocious as to rob them of any claim to human rights for themselves. If we take into account that these thoughts arose in a society heavily traumatized by years of war, ethnically motivated displacement, and atrocities, we can understand how they felt. But the arguments failed to recognize the true meaning of human rights. They called something "human rights" that had nothing to do with human rights, something that emerged, instead, from the realm of private right mixed with a kind of penal law that still embraces revenge.

This confused view got support from various elements of the Dayton Agreement itself. The agreement placed the utmost importance on human rights. It provided a firm (i.e. inflexible) constitution. And, finally, it guaranteed all displaced persons the right to return to their former dwellings and homes. Returning to those places, however, was sometimes a dangerous choice when the original place of residence had meanwhile been occupied entirely by members of a different ethnic group, who now prohibited the return of former residents. Basing state institutions on ethnicity further strengthened those defensive reactions. The combination of all of these factors made the situation desperate. Although individuals theoretically had access to all the guarantees and rights they needed to live together peacefully in a mixed ethnic society by returning to their former homes, for years most of them were unable to do so because of the ethnically drawn borders. And when they tried to actively promote living together peacefully, they were confronted with inflexible institutions based on ethnicity. Not only had the state been organized along clear ethnic divisions, those divisions were irrevocably frozen in place.

What we see in Bosnia is an extreme case of the individualization of human rights that we discussed above in general within the context of internationalizing those rights. The example shows how consistent individualization of human rights culminates in their being privatized. The residents of a war-torn country were expected to promote interethnic communality by returning to their former communities, in other words, they personally were expected to make peace. Giving individuals the opportunity to claim and assert personal freedom was supposed to promote freedom for all. This was particularly true for the freedom of movement, the freedom to cross back over ethnic borders that during the war had been drawn by deliberate displacement. Individual, personal, autonomy was supposed to lead to autonomy for the entire people of Bosnia; isolated cases were supposed to evolve, in the long run, to become the rule. For this reason many of the complaints of violation to human rights brought before the numerous institutions set up for that purpose were related to home or dwelling ownership, or to the right to use one's own property. In these cases the complainants were up against the officials running the very towns that had expelled them. And often those officials defended the squatters, who both in the eyes of the complainants and in reality were the true legal opponent. This all shaped public opinion of what human rights meant: it made human rights mean the right to private property.[23]

The version of human rights underlying the state-building of Bosnia and Herzegovina includes no element of democratic legitimacy. It was not suited to bring peace to a country where ethnically defined groups were the main cause of segmentation within the population. We can hardly blame the United States for implementing its own version of human rights (without changing it in any way) in a foreign country, even though the US version of human rights has its own peculiarities due to its very specific background in the history of that country. When the agreement was signed, no one saw any reason to question the applicability of that understanding of human rights. Of utmost importance for everyone involved directly and indirectly and for the public in general was the relief that the war in Bosnia could at last be terminated by way of a treaty. It was the subsequent intervention that revealed not only that it is problematic to establish order based on ethnic or religious groups, but that we must also question the American understanding of human rights that on the one hand denies democratic legitimization for those rights and on the other believes that having the opportunity to enforce a right by taking legal action is all it takes to secure the exercise of that right.

Human Rights and Democracy

Behind the various concepts of human rights lies the relationship between human rights and democracy. The notions of that relationship differed even in the eighteenth century, although there was more talk then of "the republic" than of democracy.[24] To use today's terminology, there were two main tendencies. One put more emphasis on democracy, the other more emphasis on human rights. Both had their advantages and disadvantages. If we start with the primacy of democracy over human rights, we go along with human rights being limited by democratic decision. This can lead to the sacrifice of rights for minorities or, more particularly, to populist democracy by the majority. If we start with a primacy of human rights over democracy, we dictate to democracy which direction it ought to take. De facto this means a constraint for the process of democratic negotiation and leaves no leeway for determining just what basic and human rights should be and how far they go. The process is limited to working out the details within a given range of rights laid down in advance. A compromise would be discourse on the theory of rights.[25] Open discourse assumes neither a primacy of democracy nor a primacy of human rights. Instead, it sees human rights and democracy— or, more precisely, human rights and sovereignty by the people—as having equal origins. Human rights must exist for the democratic process of constitution-making to happen at all, because the persons involved must first reciprocally acknowledge each other's voluntary and equal involvement in that process. At the same time, the democratic process is a prerequisite for positivizing human rights, because it is in that process that the parties involved together define of what those rights consist and where they end.

The mediating position shares with the position that favors the primacy of democracy the assumption that human rights need democratic legitimacy. It shares with the position that favors the primacy of human rights the idea that all individuals involved must first reciprocally acknowledge their equal standing and together shape the process that allows them to cooperate as equals. Not until they have found a way to create a constitution and law can they decide on the rights they will attribute to one another, and where those rights end. The negotiation process that makes the rights of one compatible with the rights of all and remains flexible enough to accommodate alterations of those rights (maintaining its gate-opening function) also protects minorities. The stance that favors the primacy of human rights sacrifices democratic legitimacy for those rights. The stance favoring the primacy of democracy sacrifices the protection of minorities. The mediating stance need not sacrifice either; it can take them both into account. This is because it has a different view of sovereignty by the people.

Each of the other tendencies, each with its own emphasis, sees sovereignty as remaining unaltered when it passes from the absolute ruler to the people. The result is absolute sovereignty by the people. Thus one side believes it must limit the absolute sovereignty of the people by putting human rights first, and the other accepts that democratically defined rights may disadvantage minorities. The intermediate stance that sees human rights and sovereignty of the people as having the same origin goes one step back to an earlier stage in the process, namely, to the moment when sovereignty passes from the absolute ruler to the people.[26] During that transition sovereignty loses its absoluteness; it subjects itself to the principle of equality and freedom for all to whom it is transferred. In other words, absolutism is for rulers. The absolute ruler exercised his sovereignty as he pleased. In contrast, a people of free and equal individuals exercise sovereignty within a framework that does not violate the principles of freedom and equality.[27] Since this constraint is already part of the concept of sovereignty by the people, it does not need to be further controlled by a primacy of human rights. The sovereignty of the people can rely on the negotiation processes that take place among both the entitled and their representatives in relevant assemblies. The only precondition is that political procedures and institutions already exist where these negotiations can take place and that these procedures guarantee the voluntary and equal participation of all involved.

Another position is plausible, which at first seems also to lie between the two extreme positions. It is based on the notion that all pertinent individuals have at one point granted each other human rights, but only at the outset and once and for all. After that they leave not only the application in individual cases, but also the further development of rights up to higher levels of jurisdiction. In Hobbes, free and equal-born individuals have transferred their entire freedom and rights to the absolute ruler, with the exception of the right to life.[28] The concept of human rights developed in the United States is diametrically opposed to this position, because in it individual rights follow from the state of nature. But the method used there to protect these rights that exist prior to the state follows the same pattern as that of the one-time-granted rights, where responsibility is subsequently delegated to other authorities. On the one hand the basic rights laid out in the Constitution are protected by formal barriers to altering the Constitution that are so strong as to make changes almost impossible.[29] On the other hand, the Supreme Court protects rights from damage through legislation and by the people represented by their legislators. By originally consenting to the Constitution, the entitled have merely declared that they agree to a "liberal concept of freedom centered on the individual" and a "pre-revolutionary legal system intended to organize a liberal regulation of property that cannot be modified by politics."[30] Contrary, then, to the first impression, this position, too, employs a concept of the relationship between human rights and democracy that more than any other opts for the primacy of human rights. It, too, dispenses with democratic legitimacy for human rights, and all the more so, as the original act of consent lies further and further in the past.

The question of the democratic legitimization of human rights used to back new forms of interventionism since the end of the Cold War is of crucial importance. If we assume, namely, that human rights require democratic legitimacy, then they are not an exportable item. Human rights cannot be awarded to anyone and they cannot be forced on anyone. The export and coerced import of human rights that has taken place since the end of the Cold War, particularly through military intervention, was made possible by seeing human rights as not needing democratic legitimization. We must ask, then, on what human rights of that kind might be based.

Notes

1. Wesel, *Geschichte des Rechts in Europa*, 440f. See also 433 and 554.
2. Ibid., 576. British negotiators found it almost impossible to acknowledge the authority of the European Court for Human Rights, but eventually did so in 1953. See also Mikael Rask Madsen, "Legal Diplomacy," 169–95, esp. 179.
3. Maus, *Zur Aufklärung der Demokratietheorie*, 138.
4. Möllers, *Gewaltengliederung*, 145ff.
5. Devin O. Pendas, "Auf dem Weg zu einem globalen Rechtssystem? Die Menschenrechte und das Scheitern des legalistischen Paradigmas des Krieges," in Hoffmann, *Moralpolitik*, 251.
6. Bobbio, *Das Zeitalter der Menschenrechte*, 16. For a description of the socialistic concept of human rights see Erhard Denninger, "Menschenrechte zwischen

Universalitätsanspruch und staatlicher Souveränität," in Denninger, *Der gebändigte Leviathan*, 249–65, esp. 255.

7. Madsen, *Legal Diplomacy*, 193.
8. Michael Stolleis, *Die Zeit*, 14 July 2011.
9. Madsen, *Legal Diplomacy*, 187.
10. Möllers, *Das Grundgesetz*, 73ff.
11. Karl Marx, "Zur Judenfrage," [On the Jewish Question], essay, 1843, reprinted in Karl Marx and Friedrich Engels, *Werke* [Collected Works], Berlin 1961, 364 (italics by Marx).
12. Karl Marx and Friedrich Engels, *Werke* [Collected Works], vol. 3, (Berlin 1981) 62.
13. Habermas, "Naturrecht und Revolution," 108–49, esp. 113ff.
14. Claude Lefort, "Menschenrechte und Politik," in Menke and Raimondi, *Die Revolution der Menschenrechte*, 253 –78, esp. 265 and 269ff.
15. Habermas, *Naturrecht und Revolution*, 118ff.
16. Otto Vossler, "Die amerikanischen Revolutionsideale," 180.
17. Habermas, *Naturrecht und Revolution*, 136.
18. Hoffmann, *Moralpolitik*, 17.
19. Habermas, *Naturrecht und Revolution*, 141.
20. Hoffmann, *Moralpolitik*, 8. See also Habermas, "Das Konzept der Menschenwürde und die realistische Utopie der Menschenrechte," 343–57, esp. 355. Ulrich Ladurner states this problem most critically, saying that the motivation behind the intervention was power: "Der Schutz der Menschenrechte ist nur das Instrument. Ein Mittel zum Zweck" ("The Protection of Human Rights is Merely an Instrument, a Means to an End"), *Die Zeit*, 28 April 2011.
21. Gret Haller, "Individualisierung der Menschenrechte?" 123–44, esp. 125. For additional background information, see also Haller, *Limits of Atlanticism*.
22. The inhabitants of Bosnia with Moslem origins call themselves Bosniaks. The European Court for Human Rights has ruled that basing the eligibility to run for an office in the three-part presidency on ethnicity is a violation of the European Convention on Human Rights (Sejdic *v.* Bosnia and Herzegovina, application nos. 27996/06 and 34836/06).
23. Klaus Günther, "From a Gubernative to a Deliberative Human Rights Policy Definition," 35–45, esp. 39.
24. For Rousseau's and Kant's terminology, see Maus, *Zur Aufklärung der Demokratietheorie*, 191ff.
25. Habermas, *Faktizität und Geltung*, 109ff.
26. Maus shows that this view can already be found in Rousseau and Kant. Maus, "Freiheitsrechte und Volkssouveränität," 507–562, esp. 545ff.
27. Bielefeldt, *Kants Symbolik*, 123.
28. Günther, "From a Gubernative to a Deliberative Human Rights Policy," 43.
29. Maus, "Verfassung oder Vertrag," 350–382, esp. 363ff.
30. This is Christoph Möllers's description of various concepts that include, among other things, the US notion of the separation of powers. Möllers, *Die Drei Gewalten*, 35.

Chapter 8

MORALIZING HUMAN RIGHTS

If it is not up to the entitled to decide just what human rights involve and how far they go, someone or something else must make that decision. Reverting to ideas from before the Copernican Revolution in our conception of right would be to ignore the historical moment in the history of the development of thought when mankind began to realize that order is not something prescribed from without, but is something that man himself must devise. Both classical and modern natural right took recourse to moral norms, thereby setting up a prepolitical barrier that legislature was not allowed to transgress.[1] And today, when not grounded and legitimized democratically, the arguments brought forth in favor of human rights are often moral arguments.[2] Obviously, it is easy to fall back on moral categories when democratic negotiations are lacking, because moral norms are something individual. Moral norms are not reached by collective agreement. In the end, each person is responsible for his or her own moral principles.[3] The only way to make morals universally binding is to turn them into law, on the condition that they survive the eye-of-the-needle test, drop their moral cloak, and become secular. But the realm of morals knows no such procedures. Therefore moral norms cannot be altered by them. Sometimes changes in legal norms reveal changes that have taken place in morals. The most prominent example remains that of legislature on abortion.

In contrast to legal norms, moral norms cannot be prescribed by an authority and cannot be enforced. Kant refused any state prescription of moral categories: the state has no prerogative to influence an individual's conscience. He corrected Rousseau precisely where Rousseau's conception of freedom becomes an illusion. In Rousseau's virtuous state, morals are enforced by force. Equally controversial is the notion that private moral norms can be universally binding. It makes the adherents of certain morals watchmen of virtue and inevitably leads to dictatorial conditions when the private guards of moral come to power.

If human rights get their legitimacy from morals, then who can codify them? Since morals have no institutionalized procedure for universal agreement, it can only be done by individuals. As "moral individuals" these people must think of themselves as "*innately* embedded in a network of moral obligations and rights."[4] One's understanding of morals is always subjective, even when discussing with others what is morally right.[5] The question, then, is: what makes these individuals special? The answer is best illustrated by historical context, for example, the ancient idea of the role of the high priest.[6] Modern, pluralistic societies have professionals of all kinds with expertise in their own fields. Judges, too, may produce moral norms. Their signs of priesthood are outwardly visible: the attire of some members of court sometimes resembles the robes of priests. However, although judges have much to do with moral norms, they need not necessarily produce them. Legislature can never foresee all eventualities and must therefore leave room for interpreting the law in individual cases. Besides following various rules of interpretation, a judge must also take general moral ideas into account inasmuch as they are commonly acknowledged by society. However, when a judge adds her own moral ideas that do not coincide with those of the majority of the population, she produces moral norms. By the very fact that they must come to some conclusion, courts are often forced to uphold or dismiss one or the other moral view when ruling on morally controversial issues. This becomes a problem when the majority of lawmakers have arrived at a moral evaluation of the issue that differs from that of the court.[7]

Moralizing is an important factor for understanding both the development of human rights and the political interventions we have seen since the end of the Cold War. Concepts of human rights can only be taken abroad by dispensing with democratic legitimacy for those rights. Instead of resting on democratic legitimacy, the engrafting of rights rests on moral legitimacy. Naturally, this alone does not explain the crisis in human rights that has developed since the end of the Cold War. That crisis is also related to a peculiar change in the traditional view of what politics and law have to do with human rights at all.

Politics and Law Switch Roles

In a passage on the origins, formation, and development of German fundamental rights, an introduction to a commentary on German basic law titled the "History of the Constitution" says that "Fundamental rights do not come out of the blue."[8] This describes the fact that policy making and lawmaking cooperated up until the end of the Cold War. At the national level it meant that lawmakers passed catalogs of human rights and legislation to ascertain those rights, and courts then applied and asserted those rights in individual cases. After the internationalization of human rights, this arrangement lost some of its plausibility, because then the political negotiation of catalogs of human rights went by the name of dialogue among governments. Although in reality the outcome of such negotiation was simply set before the parliaments of each of the countries involved, the general perception was that the former arrangement was still intact, and this was the case for two reasons: For one, the East-West controversy stressed the role of the state in negotiating catalogs of human rights. Although the controversy itself was not borne out at the parliamentary level, it was considered an element of politics, namely, a component of foreign policy. For another, at the international level, when it came to applying those rights in individual cases, it was considered a matter for the courts, even in the relatively modest framework within which complaint proceedings could take place at all, except in Western Europe, which had developed more sophisticated international jurisdiction.

Keeping that perception of the link between legislature and jurisdiction in mind and comparing it to current views on human rights, we find that today's notions deviate starkly from previous views. Today, human rights get much more coverage in the media than they did during the Cold War. They have become "a global currency into which almost anyone can convert any claim."[9] And that coverage focuses increasingly on the enforcement, for the most part through political action, of basic and human rights that have already been codified. We hear occasionally of basic or human rights getting enforced through the conventional procedures of the court. And the public is interested in knowing that. But much more often and spectacular is the media's mention of "human rights" within the context of demands for political action. Using human rights to justify military intervention in their name is only the most extreme example. More often we see the purely political act of heads of state and government reminding other heads of state and government to observe human rights. In another purely political act, sometimes one country presumptuously publishes reports on the state of the development of human rights in other countries.

Nongovernmental organizations, too, intervene in a predominantly political manner, though some are specialized in enforcing human rights via legal procedures. The trend goes back to the 1970s. Within the context of the East-West confrontation, once the East had joined the parley on human rights, particularly with its emphasis on the role of the state, the question of which human rights issues were most important for the international public changed entirely. Nongovernmental agents became transnationally active, organizing global moral campaigns and demanding compliance with human rights.[10] During the same period, the West came up with the concept of "civil society" for the purpose of providing the people subjugated by totalitarian states with a mode of thought useful for defending themselves against the state.[11] While nations negotiated instruments of international law for the protection of human rights from within the constellation of international organizations, the worldwide public saw the demand for democracy and human rights in totalitarian states as being the major issue. The moral campaign became an instrument with which nongovernmental agents (who in democratic states, too, soon came to be called "agents of civil society") began to support—with considerable publicity—civil society's dissidents in other countries. These were the first attempts at a type of human-rights activism that saw its calling in the exertion of political influence to achieve, if possible, worldwide validity for human rights. The end of the Cold War gave such activism an unexpected boost.

Basically, activism of that kind is beyond reproach, but it did lead to a narrowing of the public perception of what human rights are about. It made little mention of the struggle with the real or desired implications of human rights. In other words: little mention of the act of positivization. Today most debates that deal with such questions focus on adding new groups of rights to existing ones, for example, the right to food. These debates are indispensable. But presently they often lead nowhere, because the general public is unaware of the fact that the contents of rights must always be negotiated anew. As a political issue, the continuous debate over just what basic and human rights are about has ground to a halt. It went from the realm of policy making to the realm of the courts and is today decided by judges and experts. There is no political discussion of where those rights end such that they remain compatible with the rights of all others. And for the most part, there is no discussion of how basic and human rights are constrained by time and place, factors that repeatedly make the renegotiation of the limits of rights necessary.

The commentary on the German Constitution that was mentioned above has proven to be correct in exactly the sense that it denied: Today the general public no longer sees the positivization of basic and human rights as a political issue but thinks of human rights as if they "came out of the blue." Klaus Günther writes, "Although we claim our human rights everywhere and at all times, we behave toward them as we do toward ready-made products that we passively consume without being involved in their production or without knowing how they work. We become dependent on those who make these products and on those who sell them to us, and ignorant of their construction."[12] Obviously, to a certain degree, in the general public's perception of human rights, the roles of political responsibility and legal responsibility have been switched. The shift of positivization away from being a concern of politics and toward being a concern for the courts was furthered by internationalizing human rights and was insofar at least partially inevitable. But at the national level this would not have to be so, because at the national level we do have democratically elected institutions prepared to write constitutions and make law. As said before, it helps to look at all levels. It might show how to prevent the lack of democracy at the international level from impacting the national level.[13] There was never any pressure to shift in the opposite direction, that is, to take the application of human rights in individual cases from the realm of the court to the political realm. At best we could surmise that this was caused by the constellation of the Cold War, an arrangement that more or less called for massive moralizing in order to break up the totalitarian structures in the East at all. But when we now survey the time that has passed since the end of the Cold War, we find very different causes.

Dehumanizing By Moralizing

When we say that the *application* of basic and human rights in individual cases has shifted from the courts to politics it would actually be more precise to say that the "*non*application" of rights has made that shift. Giving a few examples, Jörg Sandkühler has shown what can happen when moral beliefs become rationalizations for acts or behavior that the law otherwise strives to prevent in the name of humanity. For example, some people "feel morally 'entitled' to do what they do, even if it means giving orders to accept 'collateral damage,' in other words, to kill civilians in violation of international agreements in wars that were never declared and never authorized by international law. Another case was the proposal of an Air Security Act by a German secretary of the interior that would have allowed shooting down passenger planes as part of the 'War on Terror' (the German Constitutional Court later declared the act unconstitutional). In a third case, a vice-president of Frankfurt's police, leading a search for a kidnapped boy, felt entitled to threaten a suspect with torture during interrogation and to misguide subordinates to employ severe duress, and so on."[14] Although he had murdered the boy, the suspect threatened with torture during interrogation was later awarded compensation for the violation of his human rights. In a letter to the editor of a daily newspaper, one morally offended reader complained that "Our legal system endorses the incredible. … The man should have no human rights at all."[15]

It is easy to find further examples of such moralizing. What we know of events at the prisons at Guantanamo and Abu Ghraib is among them.[16] And the muddled interpretation of human rights in Bosnia and Herzegovina described above can also be traced to moralizing. In the Balkan Wars, collective moralizing was behind the killing of members of one ethnic group by members of another ethnic group based entirely on group membership. It in part involved decade-old ethnic-related crimes committed during the Second World War or during partisan struggles. Based on crimes committed in the past by members of one ethnic group, that entire group was considered so morally inferior that no one asked whether they were human, or whether their lives were worth protecting. The individual fact of belonging to the wrong ethnic group made these people so inferior in the eyes of others that their killers no longer regarded them as human beings at all. In its most extreme form, moralizing culminates in dehumanizing.

We see what happens when moralizing gets confused with the application—or lack of application—of human rights to individual cases, especially when those rights have been codified and have already been acknowledged for a long time. In situations like those, moralizing backslides to deny certain people their rights because they have discredited themselves morally in the past. Dictators do not back their deeds with morals; they almost always claim to act for the benefit of public order. When today's Arab states use force to suppress liberation movements, that force is not grounded in morals, it is simply the way those states have always dealt with rebels. Morals crop up as arguments for denying individuals or groups of people their rights. This exposes a crucial feature of human rights of which the public in general is no longer aware. Human rights were not invented for virtuous people; on the contrary, they were devised to protect those that society despises, which includes, among others, criminals, beggars, vagabonds, and refugees. Well-off and well-behaved citizens had less cause to call for protection of their human rights than these disdained persons, although they, too, have had to fight for their liberties. The breakthrough was when human rights came to be attributed for the sole fact of "being human."

Acts of dehumanizing done in the name of morals shows how important it is to codify basic and human rights without specific relation to any particular case. The limits of rights especially need to be defined by law at a time when no concrete case is already pending. Turning over the codification of rights to lawmakers allows us to bring our moral arguments forward. In the negotiation process these will be weighed against other arguments from other areas, like philosophy, religion, life experience in general, or personal experience with debasement. Before codification, the negotiation process must take all aspects through the eye of the needle. In meeting that condition and becoming law, arguments, including moral arguments, get neutralized. By making it law, we in turn prevent moralizing from being part of the application of rights in any specific instance. Ultimately, if we return to moralizing, we destroy human rights.

In closing this section, let me mention two examples of the extent to which moralizing has become a part of our lives without our realizing it. The first is something that has found its way into how we talk about a "population." Not long ago, warlike events and natural catastrophes struck populations. The population was not further differentiated into the acceptable and the inacceptable. Today we hear that these disasters hit the "civil population." And there is a possible reason for that choice of words. Civil wars increasingly involve private militia units, from which the unarmed population needs to be distinguished. In recent years the population has come to almost always be called "innocent." Terror attacks and wars cause the deaths of countless "innocent" people. Their deaths are lamentable and deplorable; that much is beyond doubt. But is the loss of lives of innocent victims worse than the loss of lives of other victims that are—for some reason, or only by some—considered less innocent? Some cases clearly involve guilt. A suicide bomber consciously seeks to act in a way that involves guilt in penal terms, even though he, if successful, will never be tried in court. And yet, when we speak of the "innocent" population, we are insinuating that the disaster may have also hit "guilty" people, people who "don't matter." In other words, mindless habits of speech support moralizing.[17]

My second example concerns a single alarming, event. In the days following the arrest of the former director of the International Monetary Fund the media were accused of degrading the accused man. Most critics argued that one is innocent until proven guilty (and therefore deserves humane treatment from the start). That argumentation in itself, however, involves a grave violation of human dignity. Whether an accused person can be convicted of having committed a crime is something that must be decided in legal proceedings. The outcome of those proceedings has nothing to do with that person's right to humane treatment, whether accused, acquitted, or convicted. Human rights apply to all. Not only does every beggar and thief have the same human worth as all other people, so do persons guilty of the worst crimes and terrorist attacks. They have a right to humane treatment during all phases of their case, before and after conviction, as well as when serving a sentence. The philosophy of human rights knows no before and after; there is no point at which human dignity evaporates. Not even death robs us of our human dignity, as we know from the sense of piety that overcomes us in the presence of a corpse.

An Instrument of Liberation Becomes a Tool of Discipline

The idea of human rights burst forth in the late eighteenth century when the idea of freedom rooted in natural law joined hands with the idea of democracy, making the notion of autonomy a political one. It suddenly became clear that individual and collective autonomy are so closely related that the two can no longer be kept apart. There were interruptions in the progress of the idea of liberation, but in both the nineteenth and the twentieth centuries it was impressively furthered in various regions. Most notable among them were the revolutions of 1989.

A mere few years later a development set in that almost sounded the knell for the two-hundred-year-old liberating view. Over the last twenty or so years we have seen some countries "order" other countries to instate collective autonomy; democracy has become an export item.

Claus Offe has analyzed the meaning of the verb "to democratize." The word has undergone an astonishing transition from being an intransitive to becoming a transitive verb, in other words, from "characterizing a change of regime prompted by conflicts *within* a society on its way to democracy, to meaning a procedure done *to* a society by *external* agents with evangelistic bearing: *We* will democratize *you*!"[18]

If democracy and human rights are inherently intertwined, then disciplining attitudes such as these also have an effect on those rights. We can look at the link between human rights and democracy from two different angles. From one, we focus on the democratic authorization of human rights, in other words, the importance of democracy for articulating human rights. From the other, we ask how important human rights are for democracy. Beyond the fact that each of them is a precondition for the other, we can emphasize their relationship further by asking whether it is possible, or whether we ought, to formulate a human right to democracy.[19]

We cannot pursue that question at this point. More pressing is the exploration of the effects that the forceful export of democracy has had on human rights. They have been disastrous. The suspicion has grown that human rights are "a cover-up, a humanitarian pretense of Western imperialism and a lure of the superpower in its fight against Islam."[20] Just as, since the end of the Cold War, people have come to feel threatened and coerced into democracy, they are beginning to feel threatened and coerced into accepting human rights. At least since the second war in Iraq, and particularly after the rationale for it switched from eliminating weapons of mass destruction to securing human rights, the world has seen what such a threat can mean.

Rationalizations for interventions in Third World countries have often been based on a claim of taking a "duty to protect" human rights seriously. Normally a state's duty to protect fundamental rights is discussed at the national level. In Germany it particularly involved the third-party effect of constitutional rights—protection of the individual from violation of his constitutional rights by private parties. It made basic rights the basis for passing law regarding that duty of the state.[21] But once the thought is taken to the international level, it changes in many respects. The duty to protect human rights becomes a reason to act; it "immediately moralizes human rights."[22] Many moral norms cannot be translated into legal norms, for instance, the moral norm to be polite. And no one can claim for himself the right to force others to adhere to nonlegal moral norms of this kind. Furthermore, things get very difficult when moral norms are forced on people without first becoming law. This has many reasons. First, there is no way for the legal system to exercise control; behavior based on morals cannot be investigated. Also, the decision to base behavior on morals is always the decision of an individual, because moral norms are always one's subjective concern, they are not democratically agreed upon. Controversial moralizing turns human rights that were originally intended to protect the individual from the power of the state into a "to-do list *for* a global monopoly of power; it turns the right to freedom into an authorization to enforce norms" that not only permits the exertion of pressure on other countries, but if necessary, also justifies military intervention.[23]

The observable transition of human rights from being an instrument of liberation to becoming a method of discipline is further promoted by today's overall tendency to leave democracy out of the creation of law. It would take us too far now to describe that tendency and the reasons for it, which not wholly, but in part, spring from globalization. Nonetheless, I would like to mention a few aspects that are crucial for human rights. In the broadest sense, they can be seen as facets of the tension between normativity and reality. In a nutshell: the transition involves shifting normative issues into the realm of the cognitive.[24] This means that these issues go from dealing with something that is desirable to becoming an assertion of something merely "clearly recognized" as the way things are.[25] While we can leave the recognition of "how things are" up to our experts, clarifying "what we want" is not something we can delegate. At most, we can ask professionals "what we ought to want," but even then we must scrutinize their solution, because they can do no more than present their opinions and pros and cons, even if their final report provides a well-founded recommendation.[26]

Ideals are never identical to reality, except in a perfect world or dictatorship. Genuine "volition" always involves a deviation from reality or, at the most, the will to prevent others from deviation.

Notes

1. Habermas, "Zur Legitimation der Menschenrechte," 386–403, esp. 388ff.
2. Maus, *Zur Aufklärung der Demokratietheorie*, 310f. and 330ff. Menke and Raimondi distinguish three different categories of conceptions of human rights, although they put the natural-law conception and the moral conception together in one category and contrast it with the other two. Menke and Raimondi, *Die Revolution der Menschenrechte*, 310.
3. Sandkühler, *Recht und Moral*, 13ff.
4. Habermas, "Das Konzept der Menschenwürde und die realistische Utopie der Menschenrechte," 343–57, esp. 349, footnote 15 (emphasis by Habermas).
5. Ingeborg Maus compares Kant's "monological" method for deciding what is morally right with the "non-monological" method of decision making used in legislature. *Zur Aufklärung der Demokratietheorie*, 330f.
6. A comparison was also made by Horst Drier in *Die Zeit* (7 May 2009) by saying that the exegete of the Constitution is not a high priest. Menke and Raimondi say that "philosophers, theologians, high courts," and surprisingly, "legislators" are the only people who—on the condition that referendums take place—may convert into binding right the outcome of the type of political process demanded by the authors for determining whereof human rights consist. Menke and Raimondi, *Die Revolution der Menschenrechte*, 9.
7. Christoph Möllers, *Demokratie—Zumutungen und Versprechen* (Berlin, 2008), 71.
8. Dreier, "Grundrechte," 49.
9. Klaus Günther, "Menschenrechte zwischen Staaten und Dritten: Vom vertikalen zum horizontalen Verständnis der Menschenrechte," in *Was bleibt vom Staat? Demokratie, Recht und Verfassung im globalen Zeitalter*, eds. Nicole Deitelhoff and Jens Steffek (Frankfurt am Main/New York, 2009), 259–80, esp. 262.
10. Hoffmann, *Moralpolitik*, 29ff.

11. Klaus von Beyme, "Zivilgesellschaft—Karriere und Leistung eines Modebegriffs," in *Europäische Zivilgesellschaft in Ost und West*, eds. Manfred Hildemeier, Jürgen Kocka, Christoph Conrad (Frankfurt am Main/New York, 2000), 41f.
12. Günther, "From a Gubernative to a Deliberative Human Rights Policy Definition," 35–45, esp. 36.
13. Haller, "Introduction" to *Definition and Development of Human Rights*, 9–31, esp. 21f.
14. Sandkühler, *Recht und Moral*, 23.
15. *Frankfurter Rundschau*, 10 August 2011.
16. Gret Haller, "Die Aushöhlung der Menschenrechte durch ihre 'Moralisierung', Guantánamo und der Umgang der Vereinigten Staaten mit Recht und Moral," *Zeitschrift für Schweizerisches Recht* 126 (2006): 173–86.
17. Jürgen Habermas would hardly use the term mindlessly, but when criticizing the willingness to go along with so-called collateral damage, he does attribute innocence to the population suffering from it. When even a major author so easily absorbs and uses this jargon in the context of rights and morals, it appears as if a speech habit has asserted itself that possibly weakens what we mean by "innocent." The term becomes a "sleeper agent" that can hit when we least expect it. Habermas, "Das Konzept der Menschenwürde," 355; Günther, "Menschenrechte zwischen Staaten und Dritten," 263. Klaus Günther seems to be critical of such jargon. Within the context of abandoning human rights in order to save the lives of others he uses the circumspect phrase of the rights of "the innocent and the guilty."
18. Claus Offe, "Rekonstruktion oder Dekonstruktion des 'Westens'?" in Stein, Buchstein, and Offe, *Souveränität, Recht, Moral*, 185–95 (original emphasis).
19. Samantha Besson, "The Human Right to Democracy—A Moral Defense with a Legal Nuance" in *Definition and Development of Human Rights and Popular Sovereignty in Europe*, ed. Council of Europe Publishing (Strasbourg, 2011), 47–75.
20. Thomas Assheuer, *Die Zeit*, 20 July 2011.
21. Dreier, "Grundrechte," 103f.
22. Günther, "Menschenrechte zwischen Staaten und Dritten," 278.
23. Maus, "Menschenrechte als Ermächtigungsnormen internationaler Politik," 279.
24. Martti Koskenniemi has described the same transition as occurring within international law: "Disciplinary strength replaces state sovereignty. Restrictions no longer use the vocabulary of the normative, but that of the cognitive." Martti Koskenniemi, "Formalismus, Fragmentierung. Freiheit—Kantische Themen im heutigen Völkerrecht," in Kreide, *Transnationale Verrechtlichung*, 70.
25. Ingeborg Maus believes that this trend flows from resignation triggered by globalization. Maus, "Verfassung und Verfassungsgebung," 34f.
26. Horst Dreier writes regarding the German Ethics Advisory Board that it is not the task of ethics advisors "to relieve parliament of decision-making or to tell it how to decide. Ethics advisors are neither substitute lawmakers nor superlawmakers. But they can very well provide the parliament and especially the public with help and arguments for decision-making." *Frankfurter Allgemeine Zeitung*, 17 August 2011.

Chapter 9

Natural Right and Imposed Concepts of Man

Disciplining others by imposing our ideas on them is not new. As we have seen by looking at the transition from classic to modern natural law, even then, scholars based their designs on what they believed to be "true human nature," although we now know that they succumbed to the moral fashions of the time in terms of what "true human nature" is. If that was their intention, they cleverly concealed a good portion of normativity from the eyes of nonscholars. But to claim to know how man "really is" and to use that image as grounds for a system of rights meant nothing less than telling people how they ought to be.

And, of course, telling them how they ought not to be. In the end the purpose was to show people what sort of self-fulfillment is worthy of aspiration. And what kind is not. The French Revolution, however, changed the signs. Thereafter nothing about human nature seemed certain, and Nature herself could tell us nothing. The novelty of the concept of human rights that emerged from the French Revolution is that those rights were absolutely undetermined.[1] It was then up to the political process to decide wherein rights should exist, and the process for doing so was necessarily conceived of as being open-ended.

Today, when human rights are seen as "ready-made products"[2] made from inexplicable ingredients, this mirrors basically the same pattern. People are being asked to accept concepts of man that they themselves did not develop. Concepts of man have always been around and have always accommodated the prevailing distribution of power. They look purely descriptive but are always normative. Friedrich Wilhelm Graf collected concepts of man in what he calls an image-of-man museum.[3] There we find not only the well-known Christian-occidental and Asian image of man, but even a "NATO concept of man" and other oddities. What all these concepts of man have in common is that they exude normativity. People are supposed to believe that they describe man "as he really is." The schemes aim to keep others from thinking about mankind for themselves and coming to their own conclusions. The power to define the prevailing concept of man means "political and social power and popular command."[4]

After the French Revolution, the struggle with concepts of man became political. Natural right presupposes natural man: man, that is, "as he really is." It is one of the concepts brought into the political negotiation process. Other concepts are images of man from religious, moral, and other sources. Even the revolutionary plan to leave the definition of human rights entirely up to the political negotiation process presupposes an idea of man that could be called "revolutionary": man that continually modernizes himself. On the other hand, a trend is observable that eliminates disagreement on the concept of man from political and negotiation processes. Now these images of man no longer emerge as deliberately articulated concepts but as something that simply evolves out of life's circumstances, "whatever they are."

This can be illustrated by one fairly recent concept of man, namely, the concept of "the individual as an entrepreneur" that occasionally turns up in debate on the purpose of education and training. This concept implies that personal skills are resources to be used in competition against other individuals. The winner must constantly maximize his success; all areas of life are pervaded by competition.[5] We could call it the concept of the "competitor" that increasingly shapes market development. But a concept that sees man solely as a market competitor tends to ignore and, ultimately, exclude other ways of life. Not only does the competitor win in the long run, leaving the noncompetitor behind, he also has an interest in ever more parts of life getting organized in terms of the market.

Yet competition, we must remember, "is not a value-neutral instrument for efficiently mastering every way of life ... ; it favors competitive and acquisitive careers."[6]

The trend toward evading all political discussion of the concept of man encourages relapse to the concept of man found in natural law. But the authority that defined the natural-law concept of man no longer exists; it has been replaced by the "invisible hand of the market." Once again, we have here a normative issue shifting into the realm of the cognitive. It does not matter what we want, what matters is proper and rational insight. This trend is part of the aforementioned overall lack of democracy that ultimately means that right is no longer determined by the governed, but by a group of professionals. It returns to the idea from natural law that nonexperts are incapable of knowing the rights expressed by laws of nature, that only experts can know them. Lacking proper knowledge, nonexperts may part from the path of pure rational insight. They may not see what Nature has planned, not see "how things really are," and be so audacious as to want something.

Expertise Ousts Democracy

Democracy and expert activity are complementary. We might even consider them analogous, inasmuch as democracy has to do with normativity (how things should be), while it is the task of experts to provide us with descriptions of reality (how things are). To establish law democratically means that nonexperts negotiate with one another what will become right and what will not. The fact that they are not experts does not mean that they don't have special knowledge in some other field that may be just as broad or deep as the knowledge of experts. The key difference is that the knowledge of nonexperts does not enter the negotiation process already recognized as the "acknowledged" truth: it unabashedly represents a "willed" standpoint. Reasons must be given for that standpoint, arguments capable of convincing the other nonexperts, too. But most important is that a standpoint can be discussed by everyone participating in the negotiation process, without anyone acting as an authority on the matter.[7] In a democracy legislation demands defined procedures that may involve expertise, but the relative appropriateness of the outcome depends on other things. Hearings, for example, enable those involved in negotiating a certain issue to better understand that issue and acquire knowledge of the subject, without becoming experts.[8] In the course of negotiations they advocate positions that become increasingly better founded but remain nevertheless "willed" positions.

In this context, besides examining how democratic procedures today are being increasingly replaced by expertise, we should also mention how judges sometimes devise moral norms. When it comes to human rights, the role the judge plays in replacing democratic procedures is formidable, especially because at the international level we have no democratically elected institutions for defining those rights. Since the end of the Cold War we can also observe a trend toward promoting that kind of substitution at the national level, too. After the Second World War the installment of strong constitutional jurisdiction in the Federal Republic of Germany supported a notion of human rights that dispensed with democratic legitimization for those rights—a notion that historically came from the United States. Numerous, especially Central European, states followed suit. The ensuing repression of democratic legitimacy for rights has been questioned from various angles. From the legislative viewpoint, we must question the trend toward individualism that makes constitutional judges become "guardians of basic rights, counteracting legislative authority … because in doing so they confront the legislative body, whose job is also to outline subjective spheres of liberty, with particular concerns."[9] From the viewpoint of the theory of democracy comes the warning that an approximation or a reconciliation of different standpoints is only possible through democratic negotiation, while the decisions of the high courts tend to polarize, because they must be accepted, leaving winners and losers in their wake.[10]

Although judges do not have the same force as experts in dispensing with democratic procedures, the two cases raise similar questions. And these two functions are becoming more mingled especially when it comes to the transnational articulation of new rights. For instance, we see more and more arbitration for business conflicts being done by business arbitration specialists.[11] The main problem that arises when basic and human rights get further developed by experts and judges is that this custom dispenses with the positivization of universally valid laws not based on individual cases. It dispenses with the eye-of-the-needle process; it dispenses with mutually reshaping each other's reasons for a particular form of certain rights. Rights developed by experts and judges have no legal neutrality, because there has been no process of eliminating underlying religious, philosophical, moral, or other facets. At this point the two criticisms mentioned above, one from the angle of legislation and the other from that of the theory of democracy, intersect. What happens is that in the absence of democratic legitimacy, what is left are morals. Judges certainly often apply valid law to individual cases, without bringing their own moral notions into play. But they do have that option. There are times and places not very attuned to moralizing, and there are times and places when the public calls for it. A judge, too, is a child of the times.

This trend toward neglecting democratization has a greater effect on human rights than on systems of law in general. Basic and human rights contrast reality by upholding a normative standard, one that establishes an enduring unresolved tension. They say nothing about "how things are" but something about "how things should be." When we repress the normative and replace it with purely cognitive procedure, when we substitute "volition" with "knowing what is right," human rights bleed to death.

Depending on whom the moralizing strikes, the public is aware, to varying degrees, of the moralizing of human rights and, inasmuch as it is implied, is also aware of the abandonment of democratic legitimacy for those rights. When military intervention is founded on the immediate moralization of human rights, in other words, on morals that have not been translated into law first but that simply march onward, we normally see open protest in states that have become sensitive to the issue. In contrast, the moralizing promoted by substituting democracy with expertise and/or court decisions goes largely unnoticed and arouses little protest.

The Revolutionary Aspect of Human Rights

Revolutions are political upheavals. When we think of human rights, the word "revolution" particularly brings Paris of 1789 to mind, and perhaps national events that occurred in other places as well. But besides these powerful historical and impressive narratives there exists an often-neglected, much less spectacular but equally indispensable, aspect of human rights, namely, personal dissidence. Besides big revolutions, there are also "little revolutions" going on in individuals. These are moments when individuals follow a very basic intuition and simply say "no." They have realized that "something is wrong here." The revolutionary aspect of human rights rests on the interplay of subjective and objective elements, in other words, on the concurrence of large and small revolutions.

That combination has once again become impressively perceptible in the most recent events in Arab nations, where young people have taken to the streets shouting "freedom or death." The desire for liberty has become so strong that life without it seems no longer worth living. Life in liberty seems to come so close to the elementary sense of being human that "living in freedom" becomes inseparable from "being human"; the two become identical. Living in bondage is no longer compatible with human dignity; suddenly the choice between freedom and death crosses the line from being an option to becoming absolutely mandatory for sustaining dignity.

Very few people develop this type of revolutionary attitude simply to go along with the crowd. Everyone has loved ones, friends, and plans. No one easily jeopardizes it all, knowing that the decision to revolt can also cause great suffering to others. No one frivolously crosses the line: the choice is usually the result of a long and painful struggle with oneself and others. And in the end it is always an individual decision, sometimes made with the help and support of others, sometimes a step taken alone and against the will of one's environment. The current dissidents in Arab countries deserve great respect. And they deserve gratitude from all those who might later reap the rewards of such courageous decisions, even years and decades later, and in remote places.

And yet these exceptional events should not lead us to believe that "little revolutions" happen only in dramatic, conspicuous upheavals. No less dramatic are the countless tiny revolutions in the lives of individuals that result, after painful struggle, in saying "no" to conditions that are no longer compatible with one's own sense of worth. It always involves the liberation from dependencies, whatever these may be and wherever they exist: in the family, the workplace, or in cultural, political, or other matters. The step is particularly difficult when it means a loss of security. Every human being needs and has relationships. For many people these are mostly ties to other people, but they can also be ties to ideals, groups, or other things. And all relationships are subject to change. A sense of security can turn into one of confinement. This happens when one's surroundings become too authoritative or when one's own development fosters a desire for independence, making formerly accepted paternalism suddenly seem intolerable. Many people are familiar with such changes in their personal relationships. They can become explosive in groups of an authoritarian nature, in sects and religions, in rigid family, kin, and clan settings, and in culturally or politically oriented extremist groups that often have nationalistic or racist intentions.

This brings us to how—outside of the context of group identity—individualism is connected to universality. Human rights are inseparable from individualism and universality. They involve the single human being, a unique and unmistakable individual. But they also rest on universality, the same being of all individuals. The individual and the universal countenance of human rights mirror one another. Ignoring the dignity of one single person means to ignore the dignity of all human beings, because all humans participate equally in that dignity. Conversely, a person's individuality and uniqueness come from being human, a trait that one shares with everyone else. Each one of us is unique, just like everyone else.

These two principles of individualism and universality basically oppose group identity.[12] This was so important for the French Revolution that neither the freedom to assemble nor the freedom to form associations found its way into the Declaration of the Rights of Man and of the Citizen, of 1789.[13] A later law prohibited all corporations, disclosing the feudalistic pattern in society and radically putting an end to it. Since this also implied a ban on unions, Marx was later to see it as further proof that the revolution had been merely a "bourgeois coup." Although there were economic reasons for passing the law, the stronger reason ran deeper. The French Revolution's understanding of individualism did not separate the individual from society; in this understanding individualism becomes the precondition for social integration. It enables the individual "to see the story of his own life as part of something that is happening in society."[14]

Group identity is only compatible with individualism and universalism when it is voluntarily and can be terminated without notice and reason. If not, it has an innate tendency toward assimilation through demarcation. The group defines itself as "us" as distinguished from "them." "It's us against them" has become a thought increasingly and frighteningly more commonly found in analyses of excesses of violence of all kinds, from adolescent gang riots to ethnically motivated genocide. In contrast, the personal identity required by universalism asks that a person maintain his individuality. Here again we see how individualism and universalism on the one hand and subjective and objective aspects on the other hand mutually presuppose one another. The individual preserves his own uniqueness not only for personal reasons, but because he thereby preserves the uniqueness of all others, whether he is aware of it or not.[15] This is not to say that an individual who identifies with individualism and universalism cannot form groups with like-minded persons or people of the same background. But any group that remains true to the ideals of individualism and universalism will not impose on the individual an identity that is exclusive and prohibitive.

The revolutionary force of human rights rests on the fact that subjective and objective elements mutually presuppose one another; it is the link between the small and the large revolutions. Large revolutions cost blood, sweat, and tears. Small revolutions often cost "only" sweat and tears. Blood toll is limited to clan and kin disputes, not to mention societies that have hardly acknowledged human rights at all. The revolutionary force of human rights comes from reciprocally mirroring each other's being human and the singular dignity of the individual. The identity of the individual in this universal state of being human links the individual to all other people: his dignity as an individual is identical to the dignity of every human. And for the individual, this link to all other humans in their fact of being human is the only one that cannot be taken from him. It is the only one that never has limiting traits. There can be no reason to want to lose it. It is not only objectively, but also subjectively, permanent. And it is at the bottom of the inextinguishable strength of human rights. How this strength collectively manifests itself in revolutionary outbursts we have just once more witnessed in Arab countries.

Human Dignity Resists Moralizing

The subjective part of the revolutionary aspect of human rights has been described as the liberation from conditions, dependencies, and ties of all kinds in the workplace, the family, and elsewhere. The above-mentioned authoritarian structures that use coercion to discipline individuals under their rule make up only a small part of such structures. The use of coercion aside, all of these structures have one thing in common. They try to uphold attachments and dependencies by putting the individual under moral pressure. Moralizing is a crucial part of it. It is well known how moral group pressure works, and it has been discussed openly for a long time. "*How* can you do that to *us*?" comes in many guises. (We hear "How can you do that to *me*?" in personal relationships, where it is equally effective.) This kind of moral pressure is meant to put an end to small revolutions.

Not all liberation from restrictive conditions, dependencies, or relationships has the revolutionary intensity that brings it close to being a matter of human rights. Focus on personal advantages or the maximizing of interests especially has nothing to do with human rights. On the contrary, the privatizing of human rights as happened in Bosnia and Herzegovina truncates and weakens them. Human rights are for the individual, but this does not make them private rights. The connection arises only when the individual has struggled with the issue of whether what he intends to do is morally right or not. The point at which the situation becomes revolutionary is not reached until one's surroundings use moral pressure to prevent the small revolution. The cudgel of moralizing is put into action, and since Kant we know why this happens. Human dignity is based on the fact of moral autonomy, the free will, the prerequisite for self-legislation in matters moral. It is not only up to the individual to devise his own system of moral values, it is up to him to decide whether he will act accordingly.[16]

When we dictate to others how to morally evaluate their own actions, we are straightforwardly attacking their human dignity. Something happens to a person threatened with the moral cudgel, something he cannot explain because it involves his very worth. He becomes aware that if he wants to maintain his sense of self-worth, he may have to go the route of the small revolution. What Kant called moral law, a sense that time and again makes itself noticeable (whether or not an individual wants it to), emerges even to defend oneself. It not only prompts the individual to develop his own moral ideas, it also rears its head when others try to deprive the individual of the space he needs to do so. Moral law thus has a revolutionary dimension, even though Kant would hardly have put it that way.[17] It is the separation of law from morals that protects the individual from moral distress. It gives the individual the leeway to think, speak, and behave according to his own moral code and not according to one that has been forced on him by others.

This brings us to yet another context. One consequence of severing law from morals is that law relieves the individual of morals. This concerns the individual in his role as one subject to the law, or—to use the vocabulary of the French Revolution—as the bourgeois who wants to abide by the law but no longer wants to be bothered with morals. But as coauthor of legislation, in his other role (that of the *citoyen*), he needs the leeway that the separation of law from morals provides. Only within this leeway can the individual work out his own ideas of morals that he can then bring to the legislation process or have brought to the lawmaking process by his elected representative.[18]

The aforementioned process of dismantling democracy increasingly takes the articulation of laws out of the hands of lawmakers and places it in the hands of experts and sometimes the hands of judges. This reduces the individual citizen to being a subject of law: the *citoyen* becomes superfluous and the bourgeois takes over. The concept of man as an entrepreneur matches this view well. But when the participation of the *citoyen* is no longer needed, the opportunities that an individual has for working out his own moral ideas are wasted. The revolutionary aspect of human rights opposes this. We could say that (Kant's) moral law wants to be heard. It not only demands of the individual that he develop his own moral standards and defend his freedom to do so, but it also compels him to fulfill his duty as a *citoyen*. This is perhaps the most revolutionary aspect of human rights. "Man's place in the world … the ever more deeply felt responsibility of a person for his world" has been called the "basic *revolutionary* trait" of human rights.[19] Human rights ward off de-democratization, unless they have been defined from the start without democratic legitimacy.

Notes

1. Menke and Raimondi, *Die Revolution der Menschenrechte*, 19.
2. Günther, "From a Gubernative to a Deliberative Human Rights Policy Definition," 35–45, esp. 36.
3. Friedrich Wilhelm Graf, *Missbrauchte Götter. Zum Menschenbilderstreit in der Moderne*, (Munich, 2009), 148ff.

4. Ibid., 150.
5. See Peter Ulrich, *Integrative Wirtschaftsethik. Grundlagen einer lebensdienlichen Ökonomie* (fourth edition) (Bern/Stuttgart/Vienna, 2008), 243ff.
6. Ibid., 244 (original emphasis).
7. Christoph Möllers, *Die Drei Gewalten. Legitimation der Gewaltengliederung in Verfassungsstaat, Europäischer Integration und Internationalisierung*, Weilerswist 2008, p. 58ff.
8. Möllers, *Die Drei Gewalten*, 67f., particularly concerning the relationship between rationality and voluntarism.
9. Möllers, *Die Drei Gewalten*, 154.
10. Richard Bellamy confirms this by comparing the decision of the US Supreme Court on Roe *v.* Wade (1973) with the Medical Termination of Pregnancy Bill passed by the British House of Commons. Richard Bellamy, "The Democratic Constitution," in Council of Europe Publishing, *Definition and Development of Human Rights*, 77–89, esp. 87f.
11. For an example concerning the protection of investment rights, see Rainer Hofmann, "Modernes Investitionsschutzrecht—Ein Beispiel für entstaatlichte Setzung und Durchsetzung von Recht," in *Recht ohne Staat? Zur Normativität nichtstaatlicher Rechtsetzung*, eds. Stefan Kadelbach and Klaus Günther (Frankfurt am Main/New York, 2011), 134.
12. Hofmann, "Geschichtlichkeit und Universalitätsanspruch des Rechtsstaats," 15.
13. Hofmann, "Grundrechte 1789—1949—1989," 3180f.
14. Spiros Simitis, "Die Lois Chapelier: Bemerkungen zur Geschichte und möglichen Wiederentdeckung des Individuums," *Kritische Justiz* (1989): 158, 174.
15. Luf, *Freiheit und Gleichheit*, 64.
16. Maus, *Zur Aufklärung der Demokratietheorie*, 331f.
17. Heiner Bielefeldt calls it revolutionary. Bielefeldt, *Kants Symbolik*, 71.
18. Brunkhorst, " Menschenrechte und Souveränität—ein Dilemma?" 265.
19. Johannes Schwartländer, "Staatsbürgerliche und sittlich-institutionelle Menschenrechte," in *Menschenrechte. Aspekte ihrer Begründung und Verwirklichung*, ed. Johannes Schwartländer (Tübingen, 1978), 86 (original emphasis).

Part IV
OUTLOOK

Inasmuch as since 1989 human rights have found themselves in the crisis described above, the West alone must be seen as entirely responsible for it. Thus in our search for ways to halt such developments we must look to the West and not expect solutions to come from other parts of the world. But we must also take into account how other regions have reacted to the Western approach to human rights. There have been basically two types of reactions that both see human rights as a "Western idea." One of them rejects human rights in the belief that they present merely a rationalization for Western intervention. In this view, human rights are an imperialist instrument. No doubt interventionism itself encouraged that suspicion. The other type of argument comes from cultural relativism. It claims that many of Asia's cultures as well as traditional African tribal cultures cannot accept the premises that underlie the West's notion of human rights.

While tracing the development of crisis in human rights since the end of the Cold War we have seen time and again and for a variety of contexts that human rights need democratic legitimacy. We must first ask, then, whether and how that legitimacy might be achieved. Some aspects involve both the anti-imperialist and the cultural-relativist critique of human rights.

Chapter 10

Perspectives for Democratic Legitimacy

Future debate will have to distinguish between the national and the international level. Since human rights have become internationalized, awareness has grown for an unsolvable dilemma: Human rights are universal, but they can only become real and codified within separate, law-governed communities. It does no favor to democratic legitimacy to claim that human rights are purely universal and to ignore the fact that they are always codified only for specific countries; the democratic legitimacy of rights is an outcome of their having been established through democratic negotiation. The reverse will not work either. We cannot reduce human rights entirely to being the mere local concern of nations themselves without forfeiting universal applicability. Not only would we thereby cancel the progress made by internationalizing human rights after World War Two, we would also destroy the very heart of human rights, namely, the reciprocal mirroring of the individual and the universal aspects. A third suggestion, namely, to institutionally supplement worldwide international organizations by parliamentary statutory corporations, doesn't help much. Not all of the world's countries are democracies (although more are moving in that direction). One can hardly impose on China a system and order it does not call its own.[1] Democracy starts at the bottom. Like human rights, it can be neither exported to nor imposed on another society.

The difficulties with turning international organizations into democratic institutions have led to a variety of suggestions that envision taking recourse to structures of civil society. "Civil society," a term that did not come to stand for dissident movements against Communism until the 1980s, became a fashionable expression after the Cold War. It often goes unnoticed that this term is used to mean very different things and that sometimes these interpretations are even contradictory.[2] Above all, the claim voiced by some of civil society's self-appointed spokespeople that its organizations are a beacon of democracy creates an expectation that they cannot fulfill for various reasons. The most obvious reason is the most fundamental feature of every democracy: one person, one vote. The influence a person has on any organization of civil society depends on the time and money he or she is willing or able to invest. Personal influence is also limited by the very fact that one cannot be simultaneously active in all organizations and must therefore set priorities. Genuine democratic involvement, however, involves the whole spectrum of issues in need of answers. It is far-reaching and cannot be confined to one area, just as it cannot be substituted by professional expertise.

The lack of democracy that we often find within the organizations of civil society brings us to another, even more fundamental problem, namely, that of outside influence. In the shaping of the political will, dedicated groups should have no greater influence than an individual; one cannot "increase one's democratically equal status … by commitment, turning it [thus] into general inequality."[3] International nongovernmental organizations may be part of the opinion-forming process, but they cannot be a substitute for the legitimacy of democratic decisions. Furthermore, when it comes to human rights, some of these organizations themselves focus on very idiosyncratic concepts of man. They do not find human rights undetermined. But indeterminacy is necessary if rights are to be defined by a process of democratic negotiation. The imposing of one's own concept of man is never transparent. It works because such concepts get by without debate and mostly without democratic supervision. But that is not how to achieve democratic legitimation.[4] With respect to Germany, Harald Müller has said: "I would rather be represented in international negotiations by the federal government elected by the people than by Greenpeace or Exxon, by the Medical Association or by Oxfam—all of which are sectorial representatives of so-called civil society but on whose conduct I have not the least influence and of whom I can be certain that they make no attempt to weigh various public concerns against one another, which I can at least ideally expect from authorized representatives of an elected government."[5]

Responsibility at the National Level

As said before, what we need to do is to look at this from all levels. The question of democratic legitimacy for human rights guaranteed at the international level thus brings us back to the national level. Democracy and human rights developed within the framework of the nation-state, and that remains the level at which citizens are guaranteed equal opportunities for participation in the political process.[6] For citizens of democratic states outside the European Union it is actually the only level at which they have equal rights to political participation; in federalistic states citizens can also participate politically at the level of the constituent state, and perhaps also at the communal level. We shall return later to discuss the European Union. The following considerations therefore pertain only to issues subject to international public law, not to issues subject to European law.[7]

The internationalization of human rights took human rights out of the hands of the democratic institutions of individual nations. Human rights rushed forward, as it were, at the international level—forward in time by decades, even by a century. Because it is impossible, or not yet possible, to establish democratic institutions at the international level, we must try to get internationally guaranteed rights more strongly democratically endorsed at the national level. To a certain extent this is already underway. Since internationally codified human rights hold for all nations that have signed the pertinent agreements, every debate on basic rights that takes place in a national parliament automatically includes the discussion of international rights.[8] Although it means indirect participation, parliamentary debate at least influences how governments will act in future international negotiation.

This is one way that the democratic legitimacy of international human rights can be reinforced, and it is gaining ground in some countries. When it comes to international negotiations on human rights, procedures in national parliaments or, if necessary, national constitutions could provide a formal mandate for a government to act in those negotiations. The range of application of such procedures becomes rather broad if they are so defined as to cover all negotiable issues that may be detrimental to human rights. Since national parliaments would have to discuss the aspects of the mandate that are relevant to human rights—and only these—prior to taking up international negotiation, such procedures could decisively further the democratic legitimacy of those rights at the international level. It would also contribute to democratic legitimation for domestic basic rights, because these would automatically be part of the dialogue. A government is not weakened by getting this mandate; its position is strengthened for negotiation.[9] It is, once again, a matter of approximation. Since direct involvement is not possible—or not yet possible—what needs to be done is to use existing institutions to at least get as near as possible to the ideal, even though we know that this is insufficient. Some find the glass half empty, others half full.

Indirect advancement of democratic legitimacy for human rights can only be had if legitimation works at the national level. This brings us back to the division of power in nation-states. States that have broad constitutional jurisdiction will be less able to democratically legitimize basic and human rights, especially if the court is awarded the competence to veto laws passed by parliament. In countries that have such a system the public may often feel that human rights are awarded to an individual "by a judge." Meanwhile the general public has reappraised the highest judicial instances and made them more popular in the belief that the courtroom is "where one gets his human right." In contrast, democratic institutions whose task it is to negotiate and define rights have lost popularity. There are several reasons for this, but the worst is perhaps the tacit belief that politicians are so self-centered that no one expects them to represent the common interest. At the national level the aforementioned general awareness of activities of civil society may contribute to this. Though many civil-social enthusiasts are unaware of it, the flipside of sanctified civil society is the demotion of an entire range of politics and democracy that takes place in public institutions.

The democratic legitimation of rights suffers when parliamentary debate on the object and scope of human rights begins in the knowledge that irrespective of its position, the losing minority will ultimately seek a final decision in the courtroom. In principle, by delegating the task to the court, politicians neglect their responsibility to define those rights. When they then devote themselves all the more emphatically to discussing how previously codified human rights may be asserted worldwide, it is a sign that the exchange of the roles of politics and the law has already gone quite far. Human rights increasingly begin to seem like ready-made items that "come out of the blue."[10] My intent is not to question or to criticize debate on the worldwide assertion of human rights. On the contrary, that debate is desirable particularly because all over the world the legal mechanisms for asserting human rights are still very rudimentary. But it would be perilous for human rights to assume that "human rights policy" means only this. The central task for politics is to articulate fundamental and human rights in constitutions, laws, and international agreements. Democratically elected institutions must not leave this task to others.

The Challenge of Democratic Legitimation

In recent years, in some European countries, political parties that include nationalistic and xenophobic elements in their platforms have been able to gain ground. These parties either downplay the fact that some of their own political demands violate human rights or they openly and provocatively question those rights, as if rights were an unacceptable constraint on the "true" will of the people. The two following examples show how similar ideas of politics' ultimate responsibility to find solutions can be treated in different ways.

In 1989 Hungary installed strong constitutional jurisdiction. In 2010 the newly elected Parliament enacted a law that seemed not to conform to basic rights. The constitutional court vetoed the law. The governing majority then used its two-thirds majority in Parliament to limit the competence of the constitutional court in the matter in question. This partial disempowerment of the constitutional court was then anchored in a new constitution.

Switzerland has a long tradition of exercising direct democracy. Various popular initiatives were brought forward with demands that seemed not conform to basic and human rights, in particular a ban on the erection of minarets. Although the government and the Parliament recommended not passing the legislature, the people voted for it, and the ban on minarets was written into the nation's constitution.

It remains to be seen how Europe will react to these treatments of rights: how the European Union will react to events in Hungary and how the European Council will react to the events in both countries. Hopefully the international embedment of these two countries will promote the reassertion of human rights, although the procedures and negotiations needed to do so will take time. Prior to the vote on minarets in Switzerland, public debate favored a clear rejection of the proposal, and opinion polls forecasted that the proposal would fail. That is no excuse, but it does make the events easier to understand. Politicians that had rejected the ban realized much too late that they should have worked harder at campaigning against it.

When human rights get taken for granted, debate on them ceases, and this threatens them profoundly. As the two examples show, this is true for both direct democracy and for democracy by representation. The difference in the two systems is that in direct democracy the deterioration of rights is more immediately visible. But direct democracy is not somehow more "risky" than representative democracy. Both kinds of democracy need continuous debate on what basic and human rights are about and should be about. In this sense, everyone involved in shaping public opinion shoulders immense responsibility, no matter what function they fulfill in exerting their influence. It is a responsibility that cannot be delegated to others. The events in Hungary show that even protection by the highest judiciary instance can fail when the government's responsibility to legitimize human rights fails. And just as it would be wrong to say in the one case that direct democracy is pointless, it would be wrong to say in the other that it makes no sense to have constitutional courts. Each country has its own tradition and history that shape its institutions. Ways of working with these institutions are not carved in stone for all time; it takes a democratic learning process.

Human rights are subject to scrutiny time and again, they are never acquired once and for all. Every new decade does seem to endanger them anew in unexpected ways. Some rights are threatened that hitherto seemed indisputable and self-evident. In the section on majorities and minorities in Part 2 of this book I spoke of how law can change. In countries that have a tradition of direct democracy the necessity of changing majority decisions by changing those majorities becomes very clear. Public opinion making requires adequate forums and sufficient time in direct and in representative democracies. Sometimes it is appropriate to fix minimum waiting periods before repeating a vote on the same issue.[11] In direct democracies, these minimum waiting periods, though they may not be formally defined, follow from respect for the sovereign. But in principle, democratic legitimacy always implies change. There will always be decisions that seem to be headed in the wrong direction. They can always be revised, but we must fight for that revision. In democracy, what is wrong or right is not a matter of natural law and is not a matter of morals, it is a matter of what is brought forth by the democratic process itself, and that remains revisable.[12]

Mitigating Discourse on Human Rights

"Currently we see … a growing threat to human rights. Not only does the violation of rights … destroy their normative power; but an exaggerated claim to the title does the same. … The hypertrophy that we often meet today threatens both the normative independence and the effectiveness of human rights."[13] This was written in 1978, when the hypertrophy of human rights was still modest by comparison. Since then, human rights and talk of them have boomed, increasing the threat to their normative independence. The major catalyst of this trend was a decision made by the United States government under President Jimmy Carter to henceforth use human rights as an instrument of international policy.[14] The consequences were not obvious until after the Cold War, when human rights activism of an unforeseen magnitude began to arise. Today this trend is eyed more skeptically, as epitomized by phrases like "the profiteers of the booming human rights industry."[15] The criticism comes not from circles that deny human rights any effect at all; it expresses the worry that now human rights are inflated.

Human rights rest on a discrepancy between normativity and reality. It is that discrepancy between the normative claim and reality that provides an individual with the arguments she needs to change circumstances for the better. Human rights are, first of all, the language of the suppressed, and when they clear the way to freedom from oppression they become the language of the entitled, the people that together spell out how those rights must be. Even then, human rights remain the language of the suppressed. That is the normativity of human rights. But the tables have turned. Now human rights have become the language of the mighty. The following few examples, of which there are many more, show how important it is to halt today's excessive talk of human rights.

The kind of interventionism that we have seen over the past two decades has made its way into everyday habits of speech that go far beyond that intervention itself. Today every head of state or government with any pride at all regularly reminds other potentates to comply with human rights. By questioning whether such acts are meaningful, I by no means wish to minimize the violations of human rights backed by those potentates. But we must question what is intended by such reminders and what makes them legitimate. Compare them to an analogous reminder, one voiced by an international organization to which both the reminding and the reminded country belong. Two distinctions are important. Bilateral reminders are entirely political; they follow no legally designated procedure. Reminders made within the framework of international organizations follow prescribed procedures and question the law of the reprimanded country. This difference takes us back to the exchange of roles discussed above. For one, the reasons for voicing bilateral reminders to comply with human rights are exclusively moral. Unlike legal standards, moral standards are not developed through institutionalized communication. Thus the reprimanding head of state or government falls back on a system of moral norms in which it is already "*innately*" embedded,[16] unless, of course, one assumes that countries have moral qualities and that some are good and others less good, to put it mildly. We shall return to this question later.

Situations can arise when bilateral statements are urgently needed, especially when an escalation of violence makes it necessary for the community of nations to close ranks. But irrespective of that, it is clear that the international competition at morally backed bilateral reproach is damaging. Bilateral reproach conveys that sense of "threatening pressure from outside" that in autocratic systems can impede inner development.[17] In contrast, when the reminder to comply with human rights comes from an organization to which the reproached nation itself belongs, that reminder occurs within the framework of procedures to which that nation has agreed, and this at least lessens the undesirable secondary effect. More than anything, morally backed reprimands easily lead to taking direct action. When this happens and when due to a lack of legal justification that moral norm is used to justify action, the outcome is normally intervention by force. The jargon sounds familiar: "We are morally obliged to intervene." We have already discussed how moral norms lead to deeds and outcomes.

There is one thing that can be said about this terminology or language regime. Military intervention can seem necessary and be justified for protecting life and limb. It must also fulfill many other criteria that we cannot explore in depth here.[18] But it should never be done in the name of human rights. And not only that: The phrase "human rights" should never be brought into context with such intervention: not in its rationalization, not in the concept, not in planning, not in its execution, and finally, not in subsequent evaluation. Every warlike action violates human rights. That is the only way (if at all) it is permissible to speak of human rights in connection with military intervention. We do not *need* to invoke human rights to justify military intervention and we do not *need* military intervention to secure human rights: We already have sufficient concepts for describing the desirable avoidance of human rights violations, concepts of both a humanitarian nature and concepts that can be drawn from international law for stating what must be done to achieve the desired outcome. The fast and loose play with the concept of human rights that we have witnessed in connection with recent intervention is enough to advise us to always leave human rights out of the picture when rationalizing all future intervention, even if we have legal grounds for those measures. This is my short but decided reply to anti-imperialistic criticism that disqualifies human rights as coming from or belonging to "the West."

Instrumentalization and Activist Blindness

I have already described in various contexts how human rights can be instrumentalized. Another fact is that of transnational codification. This pertains to international legal commercial relations entered into by private parties or by governmental agencies and private parties. Besides international law, which comes after negotiation among governments and is then ratified in national parliaments, today law also increasingly originates in agreements between private parties or between councils of experts in specialized organizations.[19] While governmental agencies are involved in the generation of this sort of "transnational" law, it is not done by foreign diplomatic representatives, who would at least be responsible to their own parliaments at home. The result is a "pluralism of law" that embraces various ways of generating law that simultaneously contradict and supplement one another. Conventional democratic legislation by parliament is only one of the many options.

The problem is that law that originates outside of conventional legislation lacks democratic legitimacy and that not all of those affected by it have a say in shaping it.[20] Also, the notion of a pluralism of law relies on relatively strict penal law to keep "the potential threat of an overall loss of trust in pluralized law" at bay. The result is "a culture of control, proactive prevention, broad technical surveillance systems, and—if necessary—the symbolic ax of domestic penal law."[21] The same holds for human rights. Pluralism-of-rights concepts often embrace the notion that what holds pluralism together is a global order of human rights. It turns human rights into a disciplinary instrument, seeing in human rights a rigid order that we can ascribe at will. But that is the exact opposite of democratically endorsed human rights and blows the idea of human rights all out of proportion. Human rights cannot fulfill the expectations of this kind of pluralism. If they could, their revolutionary aspect would be lost.

There is also a subjective form of instrumentalization involved in the revolutionary component of human rights. It is a kind of blindness. The discrepancy between normativity and reality that underlies human rights is important for individuals, too. Soon after the Cold War ended a wise thought was expressed in foresight along the lines that "Perhaps we should not heedlessly spread the notion of autonomy around the world without [first] examining new objective and subjective circumstances and rethinking it at home."[22] People from the western hemisphere often believe that "at home" human rights are for the most part in place and functioning and that elsewhere they are not.

Being reluctant to question whether human rights—or even our own basic rights—are endangered "at home" means that we miss opportunities to rethink how we normatively define values. It leaves the personal capacity to develop moral ideas undeveloped, just as when no one cares about the role of the *citoyen*, except that now the *citoyen* has thrown away his own purpose voluntarily, thinking that human rights relate to "others," not to him. Human rights activists that have this attitude lose credibility. They are not models of the continuous struggle with the question of what rights are about or should be about. They become human rights specialists with a mission to carry a once-discovered domestic "good" out into the world. In no way do they contribute to "politically liberating human rights … making them once again a revolutionary idea that is true for all cultures."[23] Only the *citoyen* can do that. We might ask, for example, why it is that in the privileged West, which is struggling with a financial and economic crisis that will have a variegated impact on future generations, almost no one suggests that we must redefine the basic right to private property. In light of starvation in Africa and violence against demonstrators in Arab countries, is this a cynical question? No, because the subjective and the objective elements of the revolutionary part of human rights amplify one another.

Part of sustaining the tension between normativity and reality is the very ability to deal with that tension. The most sophisticated aspect of the role of the *citoyen* as it pertains to human rights is perhaps that thinking about the normative part and then codifying appropriate rights increases that tension. No one said it better than Claude Lefort in a text first published in 1980: "The politics of human rights and democratic politics are two replies to the same challenge, namely, to exploit the resources of freedom and creativity that give us the strength to deal with the discrepancy; to resist the temptation to exchange the present for the future and instead to work toward finding solutions that will work now, solutions that defend acquired rights and demand new rights; and to learn to distinguish these from the mere gratification of interests."[24]

Notes

1. Harald Müller, *Wie kann eine neue Weltordnung aussehen? Wege in eine nachhaltige Politik*, (Frankfurt am Main, 2008), 75. Müller writes of an "Atlantic-centered hegemonic project" that he finds conflict laden and violent. See also Harald Müller, "Parlamentarisierung der Weltpolitik—Ein skeptischer Warnruf," in Kreide, *Globale Politik und Menschenrechte*, 138f.
2. Haller, *Limits of Atlanticism*, 129ff.
3. Möllers, *Demokratie*, 36 and 99.
4. Jochen von Bernstorff, "Zivilgesellschaftliche Partizipation in Internationalen Organisationen: Form globaler Demokratie oder Baustein westlicher Expertenherrschaft?" in *Demokratie in der Weltgesellschaft*, ed. Hauke Brunkhorst (Baden-Baden, 2009), 298f.

5. Müller, "Parlamentarisierung der Weltpolitik," 156 (original emphasis).
6. Jürgen Habermas, *Der gespaltene Westen* (Frankfurt am Main, 2004), 140.
7. International law is the law that sovereign nations agree upon among themselves. European law is the law of the European Union. European law goes beyond international law in that it also includes a component of democracy. See also Ley, "Kant *versus* Locke," 317–45.
8. Haller, "Introduction" to *Definition and Development of Human Rights*, 9–31, esp. 22, with reference to Sergio Dellavale, "'From Above [top down]' or 'From the Bottom Up?' The Protection of Human Rights—Between Descending and Ascending Interpretations," Council of Europe Publishing, *Definition and Development of Human Rights*, 91–113, esp. 110.
9. Möllers, *Die drei Gewalten*, 167, footnote 37.
10. Dreier, "Grundrechte," 49.
11. Möllers, *Die drei Gewalten*, 81f.
12. Ryffel, "Zur Rolle des 'Absoluten' in der Philosophie der Politik," 54.
13. Schwartländer, *Menschenrechte*, 11.
14. Hoffmann, *Moralpolitik*, 32. Hoffmann points out parallels to the British Empire in the early nineteenth century, how following a morally lost war (for the United States, the Vietnam War) each country sought a new reason to justify political and economic hegemony.
15. Michael Pawlik in *Frankfurter Allgemeinen Zeitung*, 10 November 2010.
16. Habermas, "Das Konzept der Menschenwürde," 349, footnote 15 (original emphasis).
17. Müller, "Parlamentarisierung der Weltpolitik," 156.
18. Müller, *Wie kann eine neue Weltordnung aussehen?*, 196ff.
19. For a brief overview of various ways that international law arises out of contracts between private parties, contracts between international organizations, and contracts between private parties and international organizations, see Regina Kreide, "Ambivalenz der Verrechtlichung—Probleme legitimen Regierens im internationalen Kontext," in Kreide, *Transnationale Verrechtlichung*, 268ff.
20. Günther and Wingert, *Die Öffentlichkeit der Vernunft*, 564. On the lack of democratic consultation, particularly when right is elaborated by experts, see Klaus Dieter Wolf's essay on how entrepreneurs influence the development of norms: Wolf, "Unternehmer als Normunternehmer: Global Governance und das Gemeinwohl," in Kadelbach and Günther, *Recht ohne Staat?*, 112.
21. Kadelbach and Günther, *Recht ohne Staat?*, 31.
22. Hofmann, "Menschenrechtliche Autonomieansprüche," 173.
23. Thomas Assheuer in *Die Zeit*, 5 May 2011.
24. Claude Lefort, "Menschenrechte und Politik," in *Autonome Gesellschaft und libertäre Demokratie*, ed. Ulrich Rödel (Frankfurt am Main, 1990), 279.

Chapter 11

UNIVERSALITY AND REGIONALIZATION

With this perspective of democratic legitimacy for human rights, we can now turn to the two major strategies used to criticize and call them "Western" instruments of economic, political, and cultural power. In the introduction to Part 4, I distinguished between anti-imperialistic criticism, on the one hand, and criticism that rejects human rights for reasons of cultural relativism, on the other. Little can be said to counter the first complaint. It is a reaction to modern interventionism of the kind we have witnessed since the end of the Cold War, and as such, it is warranted. Its truth is not lessened by the fact that the complaint is heard the loudest in circles that employ imperialistic methods themselves, including acts of terrorism, to propagate their own concept of man and to discredit "the West's" concept of man. In the international handling of Arab revolutions Western nations have now, compared to previous intervention and jargon, found a somewhat more reserved stance. Perhaps the worst of new interventionism is over, unless the current reserve is due only to a lack of funds. But obviously something has been learned from past mistakes.

The second claim can be met with a cautious answer. Cultural relativism opposes Western individualism as embodied by human rights based on the primacy of the community that exists in Asian cultures and in African tribes. Another claim is that these cultures do not clearly separate right from morals. In some of these cultures, duty is more important than rights, and rights are something merely *granted* to individuals.[1] "A kind of 'anti-human rights movement' in

African, Asian, and Islam-minted countries" has been able to get these ideas written into regional agreements on human rights, for example the Bangkok Declaration of ASEAN Nations and the Banjul Charter signed by some African states.[2] What we need to do is to see how the cultural-relativist criticism of human rights is related to the democratic legitimization of those rights.

In refuting arguments of cultural relativism, we cannot use a concept of human rights that has no room for democratic legitimation. A concept of human rights that does not allow for democratic legitimization is derived from morals or from natural law that ultimately rests on morals.[3] But moral norms always are and will always be culture dependent. It is the codification process that gives them a cross-cultural form; in that process moral arguments are confronted with arguments from other areas like philosophy and life experience in general, stripped of their moral cloak and neutralized. Thus an understanding of human rights not based on democratic legitimacy will always evoke counter arguments of a culturally relativistic nature. If one country or alliance tries to force morally based human rights on other states and cultures by way of intervention and authority, arguments for cultural relativism will be added to the arguments against imperialistic conduct.

Furthermore, showing that human rights must not only be negotiated democratically but that prior to any such negotiation individual human beings must first mutually—i.e. intersubjectively—recognize one another as equal and free can soften the cultural-relativistic claim that the West's notion of human rights rests on an exaggerated idea of individualism.[4] The *citoyen* cannot be reduced to crude individualism. Other cultures are faced with the question of whether the first step of reciprocal recognition is possible at all under the circumstances upheld by culturally relativistic critique. Once again, the answer will be that the process is one of approximation. After all, today there is some worldwide agreement on certain articulations of human rights, and these rights have been given a legally binding form. They give the people in cultures that do want to attain global standards the arguments with which they can do so.

Regional deviations from global standards will most likely manifest themselves in violations of equality; there will be inequality regarding the negotiation process and later in exercising the pertinent rights. The beginnings of human rights in the French Revolution exhibited the same deficiencies. And it holds for all the processes that followed for positivizing these rights. Otherwise they would not have had a gate-opening effect. It is possible that for certain law-governed communities human rights will be defined in such a way that the point where the individual and the community intersect does not exactly match where it is for Western civilization. The only prerequisite is that all individuals are equal. We shall return to this aspect when discussing how freedom and equality are related. It is self-evident that beyond this there are absolute limits that may not be ignored even when taking consideration of cultural particulars. These are especially the protection of life and limb, and the ban on torture.[5]

An understanding of human rights that rests on the belief that those rights must be democratically legitimized is more compatible with the cultural differences that exist the world over. What I have described in this book as the crisis in human rights that persists since the end of the Cold War can be traced to a new kind of interventionism based on an understanding of human rights that not only waived democratic legitimacy, but consciously barred it, as the example of Bosnia and Herzegovina clearly shows. It is one of the reasons why the culture-relativistic critique of "Western" human rights arose so quickly after the demise of Communism that it can be called an anti-human rights movement. When communicating with that movement's advocates we must thus not only emphasize the role of the individual as of one "entitled to human rights," but also as a *citoyen*, a "codesigner of human rights."

Though it may seem self-evident, for the sake of completeness we must mention in closing what is not meant by regionalization in this context. "If only the people of those states qualified to intervene enjoy the human rights to life and limb and (more or less) participation in the codification of their other rights through public debate and legislation while the citizens of states overrun by intervention and hostile action are per se heteronomously denied the most elementary human rights and the codification of additional rights, then universal human rights become a merely regional privilege."[6]

Differentiation in the West

Within the context of the interrelatedness of human rights, the state, and democracy, we have seen why the historical development of human rights in Europe and North America led to different understandings of the concept. The greatest difference lies in whether rights are legitimized democratically. In Europe it is of great importance, although that importance varies from country to country. In the United States—at least at the federal level—democratic legitimacy for human rights has been seen as a threat. This has to do with a different concept of the state in general, which also leads to a different understanding of politics. In the United States the ultimate task of politics is to restrain big government, while in Europe politics is seen as giving shape to public space, serving the *res publica*. Democratic participation plays an important part in all European countries, though the historical development of that part has gone different ways.[7] With the exception of the New Deal phase, the United States has, in contrast, always adhered to a more or less distinct ideal of minimal state. When the people of Europe take to the streets, they demonstrate *for* governmental action.[8] That they want their governments *not* to do something relates practically only to ecological issues like dangers related to nuclear energy or to issues of armament and war. When citizens of the United States demonstrate, it is usually because they want their government to leave them alone. Civil rights movements were the rare exceptions.

Titled "Constitutionalism," a comparison has been made of how the three great countries with the oldest democracies view the role of the state: the result is "political" for Great Britain, "statist" (*etatist*) for France, and "societal" for the United States.[9] The difference between "political" and "statist" reflects the divergent ways that England and France took toward developing their conceptions of the state. What they have in common is that society is organized by the state. "Societal" describes the tendency to organize society without the state. This difference in transatlantic conceptions of the state is also expressed in the differing mechanisms employed to socially integrate immigrants from different cultures and religions.[10] Since in the United States the emphasis is not on political identity as a citizen, the early stages of integration are mostly a matter of private associations and varied groups, including religious groups and groups of people with similar ethnic backgrounds. In contrast, European countries ask that immigrants develop a minimum of political identity as a citizen. When immigrants voluntarily limit themselves to communicating and dealing exclusively with people of their own background, this is seen as a threat to integration. The scheme used by the United States under new interventionism, namely, the establishing of civil order in terms of ethnic and religious groups, exhibits the same American tradition of clustering.

The US understanding of human rights is just as insusceptible to criticism as any other understanding of human rights in any other world region, many of which differ considerably. Each is the result of historical development. Each, including the US view, has substance, but that substance is regional—even within overall Western civilization. The historical events that led to the US understanding of human rights cannot be repeated; they were unique and will remain so. And for entirely different reasons, the situation in Europe is just as unique. In historical retrospect, both worldwide conquest and colonial exploitation and centuries of wars and world wars leave European identity bound to guilt and to coming to terms with the past. It gives us today a more positive description of European identity. As Jacques Delors has said, "Europe is a place shaped by Greek democracy, Jewish-Christian heritage, the Reformation, Enlightenment, and influences from the Arab-Islamic world. That distinguishes Europe from America, Japan, and other regions of the world. It is united by a kind of open universalism, a certain relation to the big questions of life and death—whether one is religious or not. All of this, plus the capacity for tolerance, are European values."[11]

Many historical developments in other areas also shaped the divergent developments on either side of the Atlantic, which we cannot examine in depth here.[12] Let me mention only a few factors that also relate to the understanding of human rights. We shall return to the value placed on religion later. Some of the factors have to do with moral standards that play a different role in the United States than they do in Europe. The manner of recent American media attention to the arrest of the former director of the International Monetary Fund opened the European observer's eyes to the fact that in the United States the media's moral disapproval is used—and accepted by a large part of the population—as a means of deterrence. In Europe this media treatment was criticized by most people as being incompatible with human dignity. Another example of the greater importance that the United States attaches to morality are certain topics that are popular particularly before elections. It would be inconceivable in modern Europe for issues of abortion or same-sex marriage to dominate political campaigns, towering above issues that are considered more urgent or even essential.

This difference in the role assigned to morality also informs the self-defined rank and the self-concept of the nation. The United States raises its citizens to believe they are morally superior. This has been emphasized to varying degrees under various presidents, but is, in general, well anchored in large parts of the population.[13] The term "rogue state," which on the scale of the moral evaluation of nations constitutes the opposite pole to the United States, is a product of American philosophy of justice.[14] Not only the term itself, but particularly its astonishingly uncritical usage even by non-Americans, has had a disastrous effect on international politics to this day. For instance, the suggestion "to replace or supplement the United Nations by a 'League of Democracies'" was produced by American political think tanks.[15] The idea is that only "good" nations should participate in shaping public order; "evil" nations—in other words, the rogues—may not join. The dichotomy of good and evil has become so important to American politics that it is apparently almost impossible to get support from the politically minded public for military intervention that does not fit into the good-or-evil scheme.[16] The experience gained in Kosovo, the knowledge of new facts related to it, and observations verified in the time that has passed since then have gradually led to an international insight that it is perhaps that very good-and-evil matrix that makes conflicts irresolvable.

The European Union

This difference in the meaning of the nation is an issue on which Europe, embedded as it is in the West, has developed its own stance and identity. This is worthy of mention within the context of human rights, because now in Europe the concept of citizenship has developed beyond the concept of the nation, and done so in an entirely new way, including democratic participation. Whatever legal form the European Union shall someday have, it cannot and will not become an entity having a national identity similar to those of nations of the nineteenth and twentieth centuries. The national identity of people living in the European Union will remain predominantly rooted in their country of origin. A sense of being a citizen of the European Union is for many only gradually emerging. It can be conveyed, for instance, through the rule of European law that is characteristic for that level. It can be spread through the institutions still in development. But above all, in the long run, the right to political participation in European decisions will promote European identity and political discourse. All of these factors that further the development of identity are still under way. But I have no doubt that this process will lead to a new kind of public sphere.

This new understanding of democratic participation will prove itself invaluable for the democratic legitimization of human rights. For the first time it will become possible to overcome the ambivalence of internationalization. The European Charter of Fundamental Rights is the first articulation of human rights at a supranational level that has a certain degree of democratic legitimacy. The convention that elaborated the draft had a parliamentarian component, and the European Parliament agreed to the charter. While the member nations do maintain that fundamental rights remain a part of their own national constitutions and that they alone have the exclusive authority to shape these rights,[17] the Union has become increasingly active in exercising its competence and approaching citizens directly. Thus the Union must be put in a position to guarantee those rights, too.[18] This distinguishes the Union from organizations like the Council of Europe. Human rights that have been agreed upon in international legal contracts within the framework of international organizations have no democratic legitimacy unless that legitimacy has been created indirectly by consent from national parliaments. But as I have said, this happens via influence on the national government that represents that nation within the organization in question. In the Council of Europe delegations from national parliaments are also represented in the Parliamentary Assembly; they are, in other words, in direct contact and can propound positions and make recommendations. This is important for guaranteeing human rights. But the shaping of those rights is decided upon by the governments of the Council's member states. For the European Union this is different. Because of the increasing influence of the European Parliament we can expect that democratic legitimacy for shaping fundamental rights will grow.[19]

This makes things more complex for domestic parliaments in the EU's member states. The only influence these domestic parliaments have on international human rights as defined by international law is the influence they exert on their own governments, which they can try to give a binding mandate. They can do the same for European basic rights as defined by European law, but the long-term perspective lies in influencing the European Parliament. Another aspect involves the planned ratification of the European Convention on Human Rights by the European Union. This option was created by the Lisbon Treaty and introduced by the Council of Europe in an additional protocol to the convention. If this step is taken, the European Court for Human Rights in Strasbourg, the European Court in Luxembourg, and the national constitutional courts of every country will, in part, all be able to take stands on the same human rights issues. The degree to which this is already possible today has been called an "alliance of constitutional courts" (*Verfassungsgerichtsverbund*).[20]

Judges, too, can contribute to strengthening the democratic legitimacy of human rights. Once again, there is a difference between the international level, the national level, and (for Europe) the European level. An international court like the European Court of Human Rights does not compete with any parliament. It examines, among other things, constitutions and laws enacted by democratically elected national bodies, and if need be, regulations made by referendums, too. The task of this jurisdiction is to guarantee adherence to the rights promised in the Convention on Human Rights and to determine when and why they have been violated. At the same time, national traditions and social climates are taken into account. It is a very difficult task, sometimes a real tightrope act, to effectively protect rights without excessively intervening in the democratic sovereignty of states. In contrast, national high courts do compete with the parliaments in their own countries. In wording their judgments, judges can express the belief that they take themselves to be more competent than the pertinent parliament when it comes to positivizing fundamental rights. In doing so, they contribute to the aforementioned shift in the public's appraisal, leaving the impression that basic rights are something "granted by judges." Whether intended or not, this relieves politicians of their responsibility for human rights. But conversely, courts might explicitly point out that the elaboration of basic and human rights is the responsibility of political bodies, and incorporate this insight into their verdicts.

Making a Mission out of Human Rights

In terms of human rights, there are two reasons for thinking of the West as divided into separate regions. One is the United States' aforementioned extreme moral elevation of itself. Part of the American population and its public representatives think of liberties as being *American*, a feature of their own nation, and not an outcome of international agreements.[21] That is also why the United States is unable to ratify agreements on the procedures and courts needed to protect international human rights. For many Americans it is simply inconceivable that a non-American might pass judgment on the United States, or even on the country's president.[22] The attitude is accompanied and supported by a romanticizing and sanctifying of the US Constitution, which is taken to be "so much more than the temporary outcome of a constituent assembly: it is a storehouse of Ultimate Truths."[23] That was not so when the country was newly founded. The notion arose when the French Revolution failed and the Americans turned away from their former ally to bear the banner of freedom alone.[24] True sanctity for the Constitution was then the result of invoking national unity at the close of the Civil War. It was the work of Abraham Lincoln. His political creed saw the fate of the Union as significant for all of mankind.[25] It is worth comparing this situation to that of Europe. European integration means to tie in all nations, as different as they may be, and to respect those differences.

The second reason lies in the meaning of mission. When earlier, within the context of the revolutionary aspect of rights, it was said that "Human rights must once again become politically 'liberated' … , once again an idea that holds for all cultures," that statement reflected the fact that those rights have practically been annexed by the Western way of life. "Modern capitalistic times … seriously believed that deep in their hearts all people are American and yearn to be saved by the West's way of life."[26] This notion of a mission is not new, a parallel can be found in the history of founding the United States. Just as back then the settlers took their own situation for the real manifestation of the "state of nature," so today some Americans believe that if only the other regions of the world would copy the United States as well as they can, then everything will turn out fine. Europe went through a similar phase two hundred years ago. Napoleon took up arms to spread some of the accomplishments of the French Revolution throughout Europe by force. Some of those accomplishments took hold, but the emperor damaged them considerably and contributed to negative connotations for the word "revolution" across the Continent. Neither was Europe's subsequent history free of missions, particularly within the context of colonialism, when the concept of "civilization" was used to gild national interests.[27] Today Europe is no longer inclined to export "what is right" to the rest of the world. The significance of this transatlantic difference is often underestimated.[28]

The most important component of Europe's independent identity within the setting of the West is the significance it attributes to equality. This began in the late eighteenth century and developed in different ways. Though France and England took different routes, they both achieved strong statehood. In France the idea of equality was part of revolutionary thought from the beginning and grew over the decades together with the idea of democracy. The three concepts central to the French Revolution, namely, liberty, equality, and brotherhood, remained together. Faced with the absolute sovereignty of Parliament, in England equality was secured by extending the right to vote for representation in Parliament to ever more entitled persons. Subsequent democracies also strove for a certain degree of equality. But things were different in the United States. There "the American idea of rights remained (even before the abolition of slavery) rooted in the idea of freedom. Indeed, in the United States freedom has often hindered equality and brotherhood."[29] Since this difference is crucial, it deserves a closer look.

Freedom and Equality

In the history of the development of human rights it was Kant's philosophy that found the solution for combining freedom with equality. As mentioned often above, freedom is only genuine freedom if it is the same freedom for all. In terms of regionalization, the reverse reference is particularly important, namely, that equality can only be genuine equality when it is inseparably bound to freedom. The demand for equality must serve to achieve autonomy, if it is not to become a mere "demand for equal quantity," thereby "losing its grounds for legitimacy" and becoming a threat to the "opportunity to make liberty real."[30] We find here, once again, the absolute indeterminacy that is part of human rights. They must be worked out politically. It is the political process that shapes the individual freedom expressed in basic and human rights. Equality is not the outcome of that process; it is a prerequisite for it happening at all. Before the process begins, everyone involved must acknowledge that every other person is free and equal. It is equality that guarantees that all can participate to the same extent in the process that defines what constitutes freedom.[31]

A central point of controversy in the confrontation between the East and the West was the question of how liberty relates to equality. In their most blunt form, each side pitted liberty and equality against one another, stressing that the primacy of the one opposes the primacy of the other. But in principle, neither of the views is appropriate. If they were, more liberty would mean less equality, and more equality would mean less liberty. This zero-sum result can only be had by decoupling liberty and equality such that equality becomes a subsequent corrective element to alleviate the unequal distribution of liberty. Things are different when we consider equality a constitutive component of liberty, namely, as something that has always been a part of it. The idea that before people can define human rights they must first acknowledge one another as free and equal is based on this assumption. This equality does not mean that anyone involved has less freedom. To the contrary, when one exercises his freedom he invokes the other to make use of her freedom also, in other words, "to be free, too."[32] This means that equality increases liberty. The human right to freedom goes very far. To make use of one's own freedom does not mean to merely rationally assess matters just as a specialist would assess and bring them to the debate. Freedom is also the right of the individual to be other than entirely rational; it is a right to be "selfish, crazy, eccentric, irresponsible, provocative, obsessive, self-destructive, etc."[33] This list of features that may characterize people reminds us of Kant's "bunch of devils," who are just as capable of establishing a state; in other words, the organizing of a state has nothing to do with the morality of society.

If we see equality as a constitutive component of liberty, it cannot be used as a later corrective for unequal relations. Equality as a component of liberty enters negotiations on liberty in a very different way than if it were applied after the fact to correct inequalities created by liberty. The basic process of defining human rights will always, time and again—for many different reasons—bring forth temporary inequalities. It can happen when entire groups have been excluded from the negotiation process or when those participating in the negotiation process have not yet brought forth their positions sufficiently. In both cases, sooner or later, equality will at some point be noticed again. Equality is the mainspring of the "gate-opening function" of human rights and the mainspring of the desire to always renegotiate freedom. No community governed by law needs an imperial power telling it that or how it must negotiate human rights. The negotiation process itself is part of the logics of human rights. It is effective in every region and culture, even if these take very different routes and different lengths of time to approach a universal understanding of human rights.

Liberty and equality oppose one another only when we separate equality from liberty, either because we want an unequal distribution of liberty or because we want equality to patch up an unfair distribution of liberty. These two motivations can hardly be kept apart. In a society that believes that equality means a loss of liberty, the only way to achieve more equality is to redistribute. In the twenty-first century the question of how liberty relates to equality will again become more important. It could become as explosive as it was during the French Revolution, particularly in terms of worldwide access to natural resources. Almost three hundred years ago, Alexis de Tocqueville carefully described this fundamental question and demonstrated "how closely liberty and equality are intertwined, without ever becoming one in harmony." By the latter half of the nineteenth century Tocqueville was almost forgotten, but "his second great hour came … after World War Two: throughout the Cold War, liberty versus equality was understood as the polarity of democracy versus Communism."[34] Few asked "which democracy" this was about and whether human rights are merely a barrier to democracy or whether they require democratic legitimization.

Notes

1. Habermas, "Zur Legitimation der Menschenrechte," 397.
2. Kreide, *Globale Politik und Menschenrechte*, 14f. and 331.
3. Habermas, "Zur Legitimation der Menschenrechte," 388; Menke and Raimondi, *Die Revolution der Menschenrechte*, 247f.
4. Habermas, "Zur Legitimation der Menschenrechte," 399.
5. Hofmann, "Geschichtlichkeit und Universalitätsanspruch des Rechtsstaats," 27.
6. Ingeborg Maus, "Verfassung und Verfassungsgebung. Zur Kritik des Theorems einer 'Emergenz' supranationaler und transnationaler Verfassungen," in Kreide and Niederberger, *Staatliche Souveränität und transnationales Recht*, 41.

7. Many examples could be given, but may it suffice for the purpose of this book to mention a discussion of democratic participation in France and England. See Wesel, *Geschichte des Rechts in Europa*, 313ff.
8. As early as 2004 Jeremy Rifkin pointed out the efforts of European governments to reduce the excesses of the market; see Rifkin, *The European Dream*.
9. Preuss, *Zum Begriff der Verfassung*, 25.
10. Haller, *Limits of Atlanticism*, 81ff.
11. Jacques Delors, in *Die Zeit*, 20 May 2010.
12. See the bibliographies for my books *Limits of Atlanticism* (2007) and *Politik der Götter. Europa und der neue Fundamentalismus* (2005).
13. Erhard Denninger, "Recht, Gewalt, und Moral—ihr Verhältnis in nachwestfälischer Zeit," *Kritische Justiz* (2005): 362.
14. The term was coined by American philosopher John Rawls, who is considered a liberal. See Bernd Ladwig, "Das Recht der Souveränität und seine Grenzen," in Stein, Buchstein, and Offe, *Souveränität, Recht, Moral*, 288, footnote.
15. Mark Mazower, "Ende der Zivilisation und Aufstieg der Menschenrechte. Die konzeptionelle Trennung Mitte des 20. Jahrhunderts," in Hoffmann, *Moralpolitik*, 62. See also Müller, *Wie kann eine neue Weltordnung aussehen?*, 63ff.
16. For how this scheme relates to the death penalty, see Jeremy Rifkin, *The European Dream*.
17. Catherine Schneider, "Human Rights and Transfers of Sovereignty in the European Union: Consequences for the Definition and Development of Human Rights," in Council of Europe Publishing, *Definition and Development of Human Rights*, 151–75, esp. 162.
18. Armin von Bogandy and Jochen von Bernstorff, "The European Union Fundamental Rights Agency within the European and International Human Rights Architecture: The Legal Framework after the Entry into Force of the Treaty of Lisbon," in Council of Europe Publishing, *Definition and Development of Human Rights*, 181–206, esp. 201.
19. Haller, "Introduction" to *Definition and Development of Human Rights*, 28.
20. Andreas Vosskuhle, "Der europäische Verfassungsgerichtsverbund," *Neue Zeitschrift für Verwaltungsrecht* 1 (2010): 1.
21. Rifkin, *The European Dream*.
22. Rifkin, *The European Dream*.
23. Horst Dreier, in *Die Zeit*, 7 May 2009.
24. Vossler, "Die amerikanischen Revolutionsideale," p. 181ff.
25. Erich Angermann, "Abraham Lincoln und die Erneuerung der nationalen Identität der Vereinigten Staaten von Amerika," *Historische Zeitschrift* 239 (1984): 103.
26. Thomas Assheuer, in *Die Zeit*, 5 May 2011.
27. Mazower, "Ende der Zivilisation und Aufstieg der Menschenrechte," 43ff.
28. Karl-Theodor zu Guttenberg did express this view in a thesis that is no longer available. *Der Spiegel*, 21 February 201, 24.
29. Henkin, "Revolutionen und Verfassungen," 226.
30. Luf, *Freiheit und Gleichheit*, 4.
31. Heiner Bielefeldt contrasts "freedom *as* equality" with "equality *in* freedom." See Bielefeldt, *Kants Symbolik*, 113. Gerhard Luf sees Kant's concept of equality as having a "service function for freedom." See Luf, *Freiheit und Gleichheit*, 5.

32. Luf, *Freiheit und Gleichheit*, 9.
33. Günther, "Diskurstheorie des Rechts oder Naturrecht in diskurstheoretischem Gewande?," 39.
34. Joachim Fritz-Vanahme, in *Die Zeit*, 16 April 2009.

Chapter 12

REPERCUSSIONS FROM THE COLD WAR

In reviewing the two decades that have passed since the end of the Cold War we still find repercussions from that conflict. This is not surprising, considering that the beginning of what is now coming to a close started over 150 years ago, when Karl Marx disqualified human rights and law as guarantors of liberty. Once Marx had severed revolution from its late eighteenth-century roots in natural law, the stage was set for the "parties of internationalized civil war" (having divided the legacy into natural law for one and a claim to revolution for the other) to wage a cold war.[1] For the United States, the main actor of the West, the Cold War confirmed the very depth of its understanding of human rights that are rooted in classical natural law and culminate in the right to resist a wrong power of state. Totalitarian government in the countries of the East epitomized such wrong power. For the West, throughout the last twenty years of the Cold War, the counterschemes of choice were ideologies of neoliberal minimal government.

The events of 1989 unpredictably confirmed the truth of the claim that when the inheritance was distributed, revolution had been left to the East. Once totalitarian regimes were toppled by their own citizens, however, debate over the role of the state, which until then had been mostly part of the East-West conflict, gained momentum, at first imperceptibly, but in hindsight ever more clearly. For one, after the demise of Communism, the East's former position on the role of the state was understandably taken as having clearly failed.

But for another, it became obvious how little importance the Middle Eastern European members of so-called civil society attached to the concept of the state. For them government had meant "nothing but the perverted bureaucratic rule of the system. Since they could neither overthrow the government nor alter it morally, they simply ignored it and lived with an 'anti-political' attitude."[2] This led to an understanding of human rights that took little interest in the French Revolution roots of those rights. And the backdrop of a minimal state hardly lets human rights appear as needing democratic legitimation. Patently, "anti-politics" cannot rest on a notion of human rights that requires that these rights first be negotiated democratically. It would take effort to first make "room and time for the political freedom of personal autonomy" that would "encourage political activity."[3]

Human rights played a big part in Central Europe's recent revolutions. Some countries tried to get democratic legitimation for those rights and to democratically develop their own concept of freedom. Once freedom had been attained, however, many countries wanted to write human rights into their constitutions as quick as possible. Understandably, this involved elements of natural law but also the idea that human rights—as constraints on democracy—must be stated as clearly as possible. Many feared a return to totalitarianism. The state had lost credit for a long time to come, and it is not surprising that everything imaginable was undertaken to restrict its grip. But in hindsight we now see—and this is all the more puzzling—that Western European models of the state were hardly taken into consideration. These models had continued developing throughout the Cold War, little noticed by the two major opponents. To differing degrees, Western European nations had developed the concept of the welfare state and found room for the idea of democratically legitimizing human rights. Minimal government ideology alone is wholly opposed to democratic legitimacy for human rights. As the Cold War subsided, the neglect of the West European view was a result of a global development mentioned above that had begun earlier. Since the Carter administration, human rights in the United States had become "a central tool for the transformation of global politics, although this was not conspicuous until Communism collapsed and the hegemony of the United States went unchallenged."[4]

Democratically legitimized human rights assume that equality is a constitutive element of liberty. Persons that will be entitled to those rights acknowledge each other's equal freedom before jointly spelling out just what constitutes that freedom. Neither neo-liberalism nor Communism appreciates this idea, although for exactly opposite reasons, which can be abbreviated as "liberty without equality" and "equality without liberty." Both take these aspects as being chiefly economic in nature, again for the exact opposite reasons, namely, the absolute primacy of economic liberty on the one side and the absolute primacy of economic equality on the other. For these very different reasons, both ideologies separate liberty from equality. The fact that theoretically the communist state became totalitarian in order to achieve economic equality was sufficient reason for neo-liberalists to endorse minimal government. Democracy in a minimal state served to limit government activity and let society work undisturbed by the government, just as Thomas Paine had described it. This makes statehood an opponent to democracy for one side and democracy a threat for the state for the other. And both are far from the ideals of the French Revolution, as even Marx had been.

What has happened to human rights since the end of the Cold War and what I call a crisis of those rights can perhaps best be described as *throwing the baby out with the bathwater*. By bathwater I mean Communism, and by baby, the value of the state, or statehood in general. No doubt, that bathwater had to go. And the child has probably survived the tumble. But what a survey of the last twenty years clearly reveals is that the splitting of the legacy rested on an error. Natural law and revolution cannot be kept apart because modern natural law can lead to revolution. Only classical natural law remains guided by prescribed and conventional order.

The end of the East-West conflict has created an opportunity to rejoin liberty and equality, to make equality once again a constitutive element of freedom, as intended by the French Revolution. It also creates an opportunity to support and empower democratic legitimacy for human rights. These opportunities have hardly been grasped. Whether they will be taken up—and if so, when and where—will depend on the past historical development and cultural heritages of the regions and countries of the world. There will always be countries and regions that push forward and others that lag behind or go entirely without progress in these matters for reasons of their own. That has always been the pattern of human rights since their first inception in the seventeenth and eighteenth centuries.

It took more than eighty years for France to go from revolution to a stable democracy.[5] This makes the delay of the two or three decades that have passed since the end of the Cold War seem negligible. Even more so, the present opportunity is unlikely to be a small window that will close again soon. And if in some regions or countries it should fall shut, there will certainly always be people that want to and that will open it again.

Religion Versus Human Rights

Cultural relativism's critique of human rights is not in general associated with any one particular religion. If Islam today appears to be particularly hostile to human rights, the origins of that pattern lie in the West. The ongoing revolutions in Arab countries speak an entirely different language. The feeling that the relativist criticism coming from Moslems is the loudest is not grounded in Islam. The way the "war on terrorism" has commanded public attention worldwide for several years, targeted clearly as it is at "Islamic terrorism," has let Islam increasingly seem like the major foe of human rights. Conflicts over immigrant issues, particularly in European countries, have contributed to the escalation. But the spread of an explicitly Western concept of man, borne out into the world particularly zealously by the United States, has also promoted it. New interventionism, founded on the premise of protecting human rights, made rights an export product—with all the known consequences. Every religion has aspects that to varying degrees reveal its compatibility or incompatibility with human rights. Escalation has clearly brought out the latter for all religions.

Within the western hemisphere, however, an interesting debate has flourished since the end of the Cold War that has gone by different names, such as the "return of religion" or "new post-secularism." This trend, too, seems to at least partially be a late consequence of the Cold War. During the East-West conflict, Communism's notorious hostility toward religion increasingly encouraged religious stalwarts to work in dissident support agencies in the East. They were particularly interested in the right to freedom of religion that clearly asserted itself after Communism crumbled. In Europe today the debate on human rights and religion is focused on finding religious grounds for human rights. Over the past few years a trend has emerged, or been reinforced, that sees human rights and human dignity entirely as a matter of man being made "in the image of God."

It clearly prefers religious reasons for human rights over any other justification that can be given for them. This way of thinking does not at all match an understanding of human rights that requires democratic legitimacy.

A view of human rights anchored exclusively in Christianity obviously forfeits universality. It cannot cover members of other religions in the same way that it covers its own believers. Neither can an "ethos" based on all religions taken together serve as a foundation for a concept of human rights. It has the same deficit as any one religion in that it leaves out countless people that do not profess any religion at all. And yet the problem involves more than mere exclusion.

The question of why human rights in the West should now once again be bound to religion reflects once more the difference in emphasis on religion on both sides of the Atlantic.[6] During the Cold War the claim of secularization was basically understood as meaning that the considerable emphasis placed on religion by the United States was an exception in the West. After the Cold War, the ardent spreading of—particularly—the American concept of man began to influence Europe, suggesting ever more frequently that within the West, Europe with its lack of emphasis on religion, presented the real exception. That debate is now subsiding.[7] In terms of human rights, it is mitigated anyway by the fact that the West must be seen as consisting of distinctly different regions. We have already mentioned how important national identity is for the sense of moral superiority fostered by the United States. Strong religious identity can also go along with national identity and buttress it with religious underpinnings. In Europe this kind of national identity has become almost inconceivable, except for small nationalistic groups outside of the mainstream.

The reemerging inclination to link human rights to religion reflects a will to ground those rights in something absolute, a desire to make them sacrosanct. At first this may seem quite noble, but ultimately it is detrimental to human rights. Absoluteness robs human rights of their very essence, because what one accepts as absolute is a personal matter, just as self-legislation in morals is a personal matter. Politics, too, "must … from the start avoid any total clamp on citizens, that is, it must [also] safeguard the individual's relationship with 'the absolute.'"[8] This holds all the more for religion. The fact that in the end human rights are grounded in something absolute is beyond doubt, but whatever it is, it remains hidden, and all we can do is try to get closer. For this reason no one can usurp what is absolute, no one can put a tag on it, not even religion. Taking possession of what is absolute would terminate the process of approximation. The absolute can only manifest itself in each individual. Thus the link that human rights have to the absolute only reveals itself in the subjective component that we have seen as being part of the revolutionary aspect of those rights. The absolute resounds in the chant "freedom or death." It is a watchword that can only be chosen by each individual person of his or her own free will. Religion, too, can no doubt convey something absolute to the individual, because religions assume absolute truths. But human rights guarantee for the individual the freedom necessary to be able to voluntarily decide for or against religion.

Human rights cannot be protected by neglecting our obligation to define them and by simply adopting prescribed content. We have, historically, once and for all made the transition from accepting prescribed order to the insight that humankind itself is responsible for creating social order. It goes back to the Copernican Revolution in political and legal thought. It changed human rights from being prescribed rights to being rights that humans must work out for themselves. Since the transition has been made, the only way to safeguard human rights is to become involved in the process of democratically working them out and legitimizing them time and again. That is the only way, even though sometimes rights mature by revolutionary leaps and procedures for legitimizing them democratically come afterward.

From Locke to Kant

Philosophies should not be viewed disengaged from the historical situation in which they arose. But there are some ways of thinking and there is some progress in thought that applies to later epochs and altered circumstances as well, or that cannot be put to work until a later point in time. Kant had some ideas about private and penal law that today are unintelligible. It seemed "natural" to him that "a child or woman" could not be a citizen.[9] It was one of the popular opinions of the day that also caused Olympe de Gouges to die on the scaffold. But Kant's contribution to the philosophical justification for human rights has implications that to this day have still not been fully realized and that remain highly topical. His philosophy of freedom is "so comprehensive and radical that in a way specifically bound to the rule of law it even surpasses the West's list of concrete human rights' demands for liberty."[10] In closing, let me contrast some of Kant's points with statements made by Locke, the other great thinker who, one hundred years before Kant, contributed so crucially to the rationale for human rights.

Those one hundred years made a big difference. Kant was not subjected to the contradiction that characterizes Locke's treatment of the relation between freedom and equality, a contradiction that sprang from the era's doctrines of natural law. For classical natural law, the harmony and order created by God was incompatible with the individualistic concept of man wishing to break free of that prescription. By making private property pivotal for his philosophy, a factor from which ultimately even the rights to life and liberty could be derived, Locke, with an eye to the future, prepared the entrepreneur's way to commerce and manufacturing. At the same time, he looked to the past to justify the social inequality caused by that order: inalterable divine rule. Locke thought within the framework of late seventeenth-century England. At the time the reciprocal recognition of all individuals subject to the law—a first step toward a constitution and democratic legislature—was unthinkable.[11]

By the end of the eighteenth century this had radically changed. Kant proceeded from entirely different premises. The times were ready for the idea that man is not part of a divine or any other kind of metaphysical order and that the task to create order is up to him. Kant took the outward standard and put it inside man, asking him to clarify it by applying the thought experiment of universal validity. The equality of all human beings that is necessary in order to perform the thought experiment that tests for the universal validity of our norms is not an outwardly imposed type of equality; it is the precondition that must be fulfilled, the conviction one must have, before the whole potential required to perform that thought experiment can be mobilized at all. It is the contribution of all subjects of the law in their role as *citoyens*. That Kant excluded some persons (women, children) from being *citoyens* followed the view of the times. It was later corrected, and even that possibility was contained in his thought. The opportunity given us by the end of the Cold War, namely, the opportunity to let equality as intended by the French Revolution become a constitutive part of liberty can thus be seen as an opportunity to move forward from Locke to Kant.[12]

Locke saw basic rights as being predominantly predetermined by natural law and secured by the rule of law. He also supported the constraint of government in favor of general liberties for the individual.[13] For this reason his concept of rights is limited to negative rights of liberty (freedom *from* the state), and he assigns the state the role of protector of those rights. Kant adds to the negative rights of liberty the positive rights of political participation. For him it is the duty of the state not only to protect rights, but also to have a part in articulating those rights, which initially are undefined. The republican state provides the institutions within which those entitled to rights can shape and define rights themselves. It dispenses with any definition prescribed by natural law. For Kant the only innate human right is the right to freedom.

Kant need not take recourse to formerly "ideal" circumstances, as Locke does in upholding the right to resistance. Locke must look forward and backward in order to mollify the paradox of his times. Kant develops a republican notion that is entirely future-oriented, cautioning us to be very careful to "let a state of public right still laden with injustice continue [to exist] until either in a radical revolution everything takes care of itself or peaceful means can be used to bring it closer to perfection."[14] On our way from Locke to Kant we can also see that in regionalizing the West we need not look to the past. We can not only accept that on either side of the Atlantic we have disparate understandings of human rights, but that we can also find this good for the future. The United States' clinging to minimal government, a situation that it has always considered ideal and founded on a sacred and not easily alterable constitution, stands in contrast to the future-oriented development of a new form of democratic participation, a new public sphere of citizenship as embodied by the European Union.

The European Union's constitutionalism as shaped by European law has been compared to Kant's concept of constitutions. It stands in contrast to that of Locke, which today we still find expressed in the categories of international law. In constitutionalism shaped by international law, the role of human rights is to limit government and politics. European law, however, attaches a political aspect to them. "The idea of the constitution as conceived by European law enhances subjective rights with an element of positive liberty, namely, that of democratic participation in defining law. It is—for good reasons—absent from the concept of constitutions employed by international law."[15] This arrangement highlights an interesting twist in the US and European debate on international law. US experts would like to see the European model extended globally among all democracies, at the exclusion of nondemocracies. Europe rejects the idea and insists on forms of international law for worldwide cooperation.

Kant answers the question of whether human rights need democratic legitimacy in a way that fit the times in which he lived. We must adapt that answer to our times, but it can be done without changing the basic meaning. During Kant's life the issue was well known: the French Revolution answered it in one way, and the United States founding fathers in another. The US solution won out and experienced another boom at the end of the Cold War. But the end of that East-West conflict has now created a new opportunity to move on from John Locke to Immanuel Kant. It is the way to reconciling freedom with equality.

Notes

1. Habermas, "Naturrecht und Revolution," 141.
2. Klaus von Beyme, "Zivilgesellschaft," 43.
3. Menke and Raimondi, *Die Revolution der Menschenrechte*, 19f.
4. Hoffmann, *Moralpolitik*, 32.
5. Wesel, *Geschichte des Rechts in Europa*, 439f.
6. Rifkin, *The European Dream*.
7. A report on a symposium on this subject at the University of Frankfurt/Main was titled "Europe's Churches Are as Empty as Ever," *Die Zeit*, 22 June 2011.
8. Ryffel, "Zur Rolle des 'Absoluten' in der Philosophie der Politik," 54.
9. Kant, *Über den Gemeinspruch: Das Mag in der Theorie richtig sein…* [On the Adage: That Might Be Right in Theory…], German Academy Edition vol. VIII, 295.
10. Hofmann, "Geschichtlichkeit und Universalitätsanspruch des Rechtsstaats," 14.
11. Habermas, "Zur Legitimation der Menschenrechte," 399.
12. Bielefeldt, *Kants Symbolik*, 113.
13. Ley, "Kant *versus* Locke," 342.
14. Kant, *Zum ewigen Frieden* [Perpetual Peace] German Academy Edition, vol. VIII, 373, footnote. This rule of slowness that Kant calls "the law of license" (*Erlaubnisgesetz*) becomes "a statement about the sequence in which European nations—depending on their defense needs—can be revolutionized." Maus, *Zur Aufklärung der Demokratietheorie*, 119.
15. Ley, "Kant *versus* Locke," 319, 343.

Bibliography

Alexy, Robert. 1998. "Die Institutionalisierung der Menschenrechte im demokratischen Verfassungsstaat." In *Philosophie der Menschenrechte*, edited by Stefan Gosepath and Georg Lohmann, 244–264. Frankfurt am Main.

Amos, Jennifer. 2010. "Unterstützen und Unterlaufen. Die Sowjetunion und die Allgemeine Erklärung der Menschenrechte, 1948–1958." In *Moralpolitik. Geschichte der Menschenrechte im 20. Jahrhundert*, edited by Stefan-Ludwig Hoffmann, 142–168. Göttingen.

Angermann, Erich. 1965. "Ständische Rechtstraditionen in der Amerikanischen Unabhängigkeitserklärung." *Historische Zeitschrift* 200: 61–91.

———. 1984. "Abraham Lincoln und die Erneuerung der nationalen Identität der Vereinigten Staaten von Amerika." *Historische Zeitschrift* 239: 77–109.

Bellamy, Richard. 2011. "The Democratic Constitution." In *Definition and Development of Human Rights and Popular Sovereignty in Europe*, edited by Council of Europe Publishing, 77–89. Strasbourg.

Bernstorff, Jochen von. 2009. "Zivilgesellschaftliche Partizipation in Internationalen Organisationen: Form globaler Demokratie oder Baustein westlicher Expertenherrschaft?" In *Demokratie in der Weltgesellschaft*, edited by Hauke Brunkhorst, 277–302. Baden-Baden.

Besson, Samantha. 2011. "The Human Right to Democracy—A Moral Defense with a Legal Nuance." In *Definition and Development of Human Rights and Popular Sovereignty in Europe*, edited by Council of Europe Publishing, 47–75. Strasbourg.

Beyme, Klaus von. 2000. "Zivilgesellschaft—Karriere und Leistung eines Modebegriffs." In *Europäische Zivilgesellschaft in Ost und West*, edited by Manfred Hildermeier, Jürgen Kocka, and Christoph Conrad, 41–55. Frankfurt am Main/New York.

Bielefeldt, Heiner.1990. *Neuzeitliches Freiheitsrecht und politische Gerechtigkeit*. Würzburg.

———. 2001. *Kants Symbolik. Ein Schlüssel zur kritischen Freiheitsphilosophie*. Freiburg/Munich.

Birtsch, Günter, ed. 1987. *Grund- und Freiheitsrechte von der ständischen zur spätbürgerlichen Gesellschaft*. Göttingen.

Bobbio, Norberto. 1998. *Das Zeitalter der Menschenrechte. Ist Toleranz durchsetzbar?* German translation from Italian original (Turin 1990) by Ulrich Hausmann. Berlin.

Bodin, Jean. 1981. *Sechs Bücher über den Staat*. German translation of the first French edition (1576) ed. Bernd Wimmer and Peter Cornelius Mayer-Tasch. Munich.

Bogdandy, Armin von, and Jochen Bernstorff. 2011. "The European Union Fundamental Rights Agency within the European and International Human Rights Architecture: The Legal Framework after the Entry into Force of the Treaty of Lisbon." In *Definition and Development of Human Rights and Popular Sovereignty in Europe*, edited by Council of Europe Publishing, 181–206. Strasbourg.

Brugger, Winfried, Ulfrid Neumann, and Stephan Kirste, eds. 2008. *Rechtsphilosophie im 21. Jahrhundert*. Frankfurt am Main.

Brunkhorst, Hauke. 1996. "Paradigmenwechsel im Völkerrecht? Lehren aus Bosnien." In *Frieden durch Recht. Kants Friedensidee und das Problem einer neuen Weltordnung*, edited by Matthias Lutz-Bachmann and James Bohmann, 251–71. Frankfurt am Main.

———. 1999. "Menschenrechte und Souveränität—ein Dilemma?" In *Recht auf Menschenrechte. Menschenrechte, Demokratie und internationale Politik*, edited by Hauke Brunkhorst, Wolfgang R. Köhler, and Matthias Lutz-Bachmann: 157–175. Frankfurt am Main.

———. 2009, ed. *Demokratie in der Weltgesellschaft*. Baden-Baden.

Brunkhorst, Hauke, and Peter Niesen, eds. 1999. *Das Recht der Republik*. Frankfurt am Main.

Brunkhorst, Hauke, Wolfgang R. Köhler, and Matthias Lutz-Bachmann, eds. 1999. *Recht auf Menschenrechte. Menschenrechte, Demokratie und internationale Politik*. Frankfurt am Main.

Council of Europe Publishing, ed. 2011. *Definition and Development of Human Rights and Popular Sovereignty in Europe: Science and Technique of Democracy* no. 49, Strasbourg.

Deitelhoff, Nicole, and Jens Steffek, eds. 2009. *Was bleibt vom Staat? Demokratie, Recht und Verfassung im globalen Zeitalter*. Frankfurt am Main / New York.

Dellavalle, Sergio. 2011. "'From Above [top down]' or 'From the Bottom Up'? The Protection of Human Rights—Between Descending and Ascending Interpretations." In *Definition and Development of Human Rights and Popular Sovereignty in Europe*, edited by Council of Europe Publishing, 91–113. Strasbourg.

Denninger, Erhard. 1990. *Der gebändigte Leviathan*. Baden-Baden.

———. 2005. "Recht, Gewalt und Moral—ihr Verhältnis in nachwestfälischer Zeit. Ein Bericht." *Kritische Justiz*: 359–69.

Dippel, Horst. 1987. "Die Sicherung der Freiheit. Limited Government versus Volkssouveränität in den frühen USA." In *Grund- und Freiheitsrechte von der ständischen zur spätbürgerlichen Gesellschaft*, edited by Günter Birtsch, 135–57. Göttingen.

———. 2006. *Amerikanische Verfassung: Der Mythos von den selbstverständlichen Wahrheiten*. Kassel. http://kobra.bibliothek.uni-kassel.de/handle/urn:nbn:de:hebis:34-2006062313641

Dreier, Horst. 2004. "Grundrechte." In *Grundgesetz Kommentar*, vol. I, Preamble, article 1–19, Tübingen.

Eckert, Andreas. 2010. "Afrikanische Nationalisten und die Frage der Menschenrechte von den 1940er bis zu den 1970er Jahren." In *Moralpolitik. Geschichte der Menschenrechte im 20. Jahrhundert*, edited by Stefan-Ludwig Hoffmann, 312–36. Göttingen.

Eppler, Erhard. 2009. *Der Politik aufs Maul geschaut. Kleines Wörterbuch zum öffentlichen Sprachgebrauch*. Bonn.

Euchner, Walter. 1967. *John Locke, Zwei Abhandlungen über die Regierung*. Frankfurt am Main.

———. 1979. *Naturrecht und Politik bei John Locke*. Frankfurt am Main.

Fraenkel, Ernst. 1976. *Das amerikanische Regierungssystem*. Opladen.

Fröbel, Julius. 1850. *System der sozialen Politik*, second edition of *Neuen Politik*, Part Two, Leipzig.

Gosepath, Stefan and Georg Lohmann 1998. *Philosophie der Menschenrechte*. Frankfurt am Main.

Gouges, Olympe de. 2011. "Die Rechte der Frau und Bürgerin." In *Die Revolution der Menschenrechte. Grundlegende Texte zu einem neuen Begriff des Politischen*, edited by Christoph Menke and Francesca Raimondi, 54–57. Berlin.

Graf, Friedrich Wilhelm. 2009. *Missbrauchte Götter. Zum Menschenbilderstreit in der Moderne*. Munich.

Grimm, Dieter. 1970. "Europäisches Naturrecht und Amerikanische Revolution. Die Verwandlung politischer Philosophie in politische Techne." *IUS Commune*. Publications of the Max-Planck Institute for European Legal History. Frankfurt am Main: 120–151.

Günther, Klaus. 1994. "Diskurstheorie des Rechts oder Naturrecht in diskurstheoretischem Gewande?" *Kritische Justiz* 27: 470–87.

———. 2001. "Rechtspluralismus und universaler Code der Legalität: Globalisierung als rechtstheoretisches Problem." In *Die Öffentlichkeit der Vernunft und die Vernunft der Öffentlichkeit. Festschrift für Jürgen Habermas*, edited by Klaus Günther and Lutz Wingert, 539–567. Frankfurt am Main.

———. 2008. "Liberale und diskurstheoretische Deutung der Menschenrechte." In *Rechtsphilosophie im 21. Jahrhundert*, edited by Winfried Brugger, Ulfrid Neumann, and Stephan Kirste, 338–59. Frankfurt am Main.

———. 2009. "Menschenrechte zwischen Staaten und Dritten: Vom vertikalen zum horizontalen Verständnis der Menschenrechte." In *Was bleibt vom Staat? Demokratie, Recht und Verfassung im globalen Zeitalter*, edited by Nicole Deitelhoff and Jens Steffek, 259–80. Frankfurt am Main/New York.

———. 2011. "From a Gubernative to a Deliberative Human Rights Policy Definition, and Further Development of Human Rights as an Act of Collective Self-determination." In *Definition and Development of Human Rights and Popular Sovereignty in Europe*, edited by Council of Europe Publishing, 35–45. Strasbourg.

Günther, Klaus, and Lutz Wingert, eds. 2001. *Die Öffentlichkeit der Vernunft und die Vernunft der Öffentlichkeit. Festschrift für Jürgen Habermas*. Frankfurt am Main.

Häberle, Peter. 1987. "Die Menschenwürde als Grundlage der staatlichen Gemeinschaft." In *Handbuch des Staatsrechts*, vol. 1, edited by Josef Isensee and Paul Kirchhof, Heidelberg, 1987.

Habermas, Jürgen. 1989. "Ist der Herzschlag der Revolution zum Stillstand gekommen? Volkssouveränität als Verfahren. Ein normativer Begriff der Öffentlichkeit?" In *Die Ideen von 1789 in der deutschen Rezeption*, a publication of the Forum für Philosophie Bad Homburg, Frankfurt am Main: 7–36.

———. 1994. *Faktizität und Geltung. Beiträge zur Diskurstheorie des Rechts und des demokratischen Rechtsstaates*. Frankfurt am Main.

———. 1996. *Die Einbeziehung des Anderen. Studien zur politischen Theorie*. Frankfurt am Main.

———. 1999. "Zur Legitimation der Menschenrechte." In *Das Recht der Republik*, ed. Hauke Brunkhorst and Peter Niesen, 386–403. Frankfurt am Main.

———. 2004. *Der gespaltene Westen*. Frankfurt am Main.

———. 2010. "Das Konzept der Menschenwürde und die realistische Utopie der Menschenrechte." *Deutsche Zeitschrift für Philosophie* 3: 343–57.

———. 2011. "Naturrecht und Revolution." In *Die Revolution der Menschenrechte. Grundlegende Texte zu einem neuen Begriff des Politischen*, edited by Christoph Menke and Francesca Raimondi, 108–49. Berlin.

———. 2011. "Über den internen Zusammenhang von Rechtsstaat und Demokratie." In *Die Revolution der Menschenrechte. Grundlegende Texte zu einem neuen Begriff des Politischen*, edited by Christoph Menke and Francesca Raimondi, 442–53. Berlin.

Haller, Gret. 2002. *Die Grenzen der Solidarität. Europa und die USA im Umgang mit Staat, Nation und Religion*. Berlin.

———. 2005. *Politik der Götter. Europa und der neue Fundamentalismus*. Berlin.

———. 2006. "Die Aushöhlung der Menschenrechte durch ihre 'Moralisierung', Guantánmo und der Umgang der Vereinigten Staaten mit Recht und Moral," *Zeitschrift für Schweizerisches Recht* 126: 173–86.

———. 2007. *Limits of Atlanticism. Perceptions of State, Nation and Religion in Europe and the United States*, translated from German by Alan Nothnagle. New York.

———. 2010. "Individualisierung der Menschenrechte? Die kollektive—demokratische—Dimension der Menschenrechte und ihre Bedeutung für Integrationsprozesse, illustriert durch das Beispiel des State-Building in Bosnien & Herzegowina." *Zeitschrift für Rechtssoziologie* 31: 123–44.

———. 2011. "Introduction." In *Definition and Development of Human Rights and Popular Sovereignty in Europe*, edited by Council of Europe Publishing, 9–31. Strasbourg.

Haller, Gret, Klaus Günther, and Ulfrid Neumann, eds. 2011. *Menschenrechte und Volkssouveränität in Europa. Gerichte als Vormund der Demokratie?* Frankfurt / New York.

Henkin, Louis. 1994. "Revolutionen und Verfassungen." In *Zum Begriff der Verfassung*, edited by Ulrich K. Preuss, 213–47. Frankfurt am Main.

Hildermeier, Manfred, Jürgen Kocka, and Christoph Conrad, eds. 2000. *Europäische Zivilgesellschaft in Ost und West*. Frankfurt am Main / New York.

Hobbes, Thomas. 2010. *"Leviathan" oder Stoff, Form und Gewalt eines kirchlichen und bürgerlichen Staates*, first edition 1651, German translation by Jacob Peter Mayer, Stuttgart.

Hoffmann, Stefan-Ludwig. 2010. "Einführung. Zur Genealogie der Menschenrechte." In *Moralpolitik. Geschichte der Menschenrechte im 20. Jahrhundert*, edited by Stefan-Ludwig Hofmann, 7–37. Göttingen.

———. 2010, ed. *Moralpolitik. Geschichte der Menschenrechte im 20. Jahrhundert*. Göttingen.

Hofmann, Hasso. 1988. "Zur Herkunft von Menschenrechtserklärungen." *Juristische Schulung:* 841–48.

———. 1989. "Grundrechte 1789—1949—1989." *Neue Juristische Wochenschrift:* 3177–87.

———. 1992. "Menschenrechtliche Autonomieansprüche—Zum politischen Gehalt der Menschenrechtserklärungen" *Juristen Zeitung:* 165–73.

———. 1993. "Die versprochene Menschenwürde." *Archiv des öffentlichen Rechts:* 353–77.

———. 1995. "Geschichtlichkeit und Universalitätsanspruch des Rechtsstaats." *Juristen Zeitung* 1: 1–32.

———. 2007. "Auctoritas, non veritas, facit legem?" In *Souveränität, Recht, Moral. Die Grundlagen politischer Gemeinschaft*, edited by Tine Stein, Hubertus Buchstein, and Claus Offe, 19–24. Frankfurt am Main / New York.

Hofmann, Rainer. 2011. "Modernes Investitionsschutzrecht—Ein Beispiel für entstaatlichte Setzung und Durchsetzung von Recht." In *Recht ohne Staat? Zur Normativität nichtstaatlicher Rechtsetzung*, edited by Stefan Kadelbach and Klaus Günther, 119–45. Frankfurt am Main/New York.

Hollerbach, Alexander, Werner Maihofer, and Thomas Würtenberger, eds. 1972. *Mensch und Recht. Festschrift für Erik Wolf zum 70. Geburtstag*. Frankfurt am Main.

Irrlitz, Gerd. 2002. *Kant Handbuch. Leben und Werk*. Stuttgart / Weimar.

Isensee, Josef and Paul Kirchhof (ed.) 1987, Handbuch des Staatsrechts, vol. 1. Heidelberg.

Kälin, Walter, and Jörg Künzli. 2005. *Universeller Menschenrechtsschutz*. Basel / Geneva / Munich.

Kadelbach, Stefan, and Klaus Günther, eds. 2011. *Recht ohne Staat? Zur Normativität nichtstaatlicher Rechtsetzung*. Frankfurt am Main / New York.

Kadelbach, Stefan and Parinas Parhisi, eds. 2007. *Die Freiheit der Religion im europäischen Verfassungsrecht*. Baden-Baden.

Kant, Immanuel. 1764. *Bemerkungen zu den Beobachtungen über das Gefühl des Schönen und Erhabenen* [Observations on the Feeling of the Beautiful and Sublime], autograph from Kant's remaining papers. German Academy Edition Vol. XX. Berlin / New York.

______. 1785. *Grundlegung zur Metaphysik der Sitten* [Foundation of the Metaphysics of Morals], German Academy Edition, Vol. IV. Berlin / New York.

———. 1788. *Kritik der praktischen Vernunft* [Critique of Practical Reason], German Academy Edition, Vol. V. Berlin /New York.

———. 1793. *Die Religion innerhalb der Grenzen der bloßen Vernunft* [Religion within the Limits of Reason Alone], German Academy Edition Vol. VI. Berlin / New York.

———. 1793. *Über den Gemeinspruch: Das mag in der Theorie richtig sein, taugt aber nicht für die Praxis* [On the Adage: That might be right in theory, but won't work in practice], German Academy Edition, Vol. VIII. Berlin / New York.

———. 1795. *Zum ewigen Frieden* [Perpetual Peace], German Academy Edition, Vol. VIII. Berlin / New York.

———. 1797. *Metaphysik der Sitten* [Metaphysics of Morals], German Academy Edition, Vol. VI. Berlin / New York.

Kaufmann, Arthur, Winfried Hassemer, and Ulfrid Neumann, eds. 2011. *Einführung in die Rechtsphilosophie und Rechtstheorie der Gegenwart*. Heidelberg.

Kersting, Wolfgang. 2004. *Kant über Recht*. Paderborn.

Kervégan, Jean-François. 2010. "Gibt es moralische Rechte?" In *Recht und Moral*, edited by Hans Jörg Sandkühler, 49–61. Hamburg.

Klose, Fabian. 2010. "Menschenrechte, der koloniale Ausnahmezustand und die Radikalisierung der Gewalt." In *Moralpolitik. Geschichte der Menschenrechte im 20. Jahrhundert*, edited by Stefan-Ludwig Hofmann, 256–284. Göttingen.

Koskenniemi, Martti. 2008. "Formalismus, Fragmentierung. Freiheit—Kantische Themen im heutigen Völkerrecht." In *Transnationale Verrechtlichung. Nationale Demokratien im Kontext globaler Politik*, edited by Regina Kreide, 65–89. Frankfurt am Main.

Kreide, Regina. 2008. *Globale Politik und Menschenrechte. Macht und Ohnmacht eines politischen Instruments*. Frankfurt am Main.

———. 2008. "Ambivalenz der Verrechtlichung—Probleme legitimen Regierens im internationalen Kontext." In *Globale Politik und Menschenrechte. Macht und Ohnmacht eines politischen Instruments*, edited by Regina Kreide, 260–294. Frankfurt am Main.

———.2008, ed. *Transnationale Verrechtlichung. Nationale Demokratien im Kontext globaler Politik*. Frankfurt / New York.

Kreide, Regina, and Andreas Niederberger, eds. 2010. *Staatliche Souveränität und transnationales Recht*. Mering bei Augsburg.

Kroeschel, K., ed. 1983. *Gerichtslaubenvorträge—zum 75. Geburtstag von Hans Thieme*. Sigmaringen.

Ladwig, Bernd. 2007. "Das Recht der Souveränität und seine Grenzen." In *Souveränität, Recht, Moral. Die Grundlagen politischer Gemeinschaft*, edited by Tine Stein, Hubertus Buchstein, and Claus Offe, 280–295. Frankfurt am Main / New York.

Lefort, Claude. 1990. "Menschenrechte und Politik." In *Autonome Gesellschaft und libertäre Demokratie*, ed. Ulrich Rödel, 239–80. Frankfurt am Main.

———. 2011. "Menschenrechte und Politik." In *Die Revolution der Menschenrechte. Grundlegende Texte zu einem neuen Begriff des Politischen*, edited by Christoph Menke and Francesca Raimondi, 253–78. Berlin. (Partial reprint from Lefort, 1990.)

Ley, Isabelle. 2009. "Kant *versus* Locke: Europarechtlicher und völkerrechtlicher Konstitutionalismus im Vergleich." *Zeitschrift für ausländisches öffentliches Recht und Völkerrecht* 2: 317–45.

Locke, John. 2003. *Über die Regierung* [The Second Treatise of Government], first edition from 1689 translated into German by Dorothee Tidow and Peter Cornelius Mayer-Tasch, eds., Stuttgart.

Lohmann, Georg. 1998. "Menschenrechte zwischen Moral und Recht." In *Philosophie der Menschenrechte*, edited by Stefan Gosepath and Georg Lohmann, 62–95. Frankfurt am Main.

———. 2005. "Die Menschenrechte: unteilbar und gleichgewichtig?" In *Die Menschenrechte: unteilbar und gleichgewichtig?*, edited by Georg Lohmann, Stefan Gosepath, et al., 5–20. Potsdam.

———. 2010. "Zur moralischen, juridischen und politischen Dimension der Menschenrechte." In *Recht und Moral,* edited by Hans Jörg Sandkühler, 135–50. Hamburg.

Lohmann, Georg, Stefan Gosepath, et.al, eds. 2005. *Die Menschenrechte: unteilbar und gleichgewichtig?* Potsdam.

Luf, Gerhard. 1978. *Freiheit und Gleichheit. Die Aktualität im politischen Denken Kants*. Vienna / New York.

Lutz-Bachmann, Matthias, and James Bohmann, eds. 1996. *Frieden durch Recht. Kants Friedensidee und das Problem einer neuen Weltordnung*. Frankfurt am Main.

Madsen, Mikael Rask. 2010. "Legal Diplomacy. Die europäische Menschenrechtskonvention und der Kalte Krieg." In *Moralpolitik. Geschichte der Menschenrechte im 20. Jahrhundert,* edited by Stefan-Ludwig Hoffmann, 169–95. Göttingen.

Marx, Karl .1961. *Zur Judenfrage,* essay first printed in 1844, reprinted in: Marx / Engels, Collected Works, Vol. 1, Berlin, 347–77.

Marx, Karl, and Friedrich Engels. 1981. *Die deutsche Ideologie,* first printed in 1845/46, reprinted in Collected Works, Vol. 3, Berlin.

Maurer, Hartmut. 1999. "Idee und Wirklichkeit der Grundrechte." *Juristen Zeitung* 14: 689–97.

Maus, Ingeborg. 1994. *Zur Aufklärung der Demokratietheorie. Rechts- und demokratietheoretische Überlegungen im Anschluss an Kant*. Frankfurt am Main.

———. 1994. "'Volk' und 'Nation' im Denken der Aufklärung." *Blätter für deutsche und internationale Politik* 5: 602–12.

———. 1995. "Freiheitsrechte und Volkssouveränität. Zu Jürgen Habermas Rekonstruktion des System des Rechts." *Rechtstheorie* 26: 507–62.

———. 1999. "Menschenrechte als Ermächtigungsnormen internationaler Politik oder: der zerstörte Zusammenhang von Menschenrechten und Demokratie." In *Recht auf Menschenrechte. Menschenrechte, Demokratie und internationale Politik,* edited by Hauke Brunkhorst, Wolfgang R. Köhler, and Matthias Lutz-Bachmann, 276–92. Frankfurt am Main.

———. 2007. "Verfassung oder Vertrag. Zur Verrechtlichung globaler Politik." In *Anarchie der kommunikativen Freiheit. Jürgen Habermas und die Theorie der internationalen Politik,* edited by Peter Niesen and Benjamin Herborth, 350–382. Frankfurt am Main.

———. 2010. "Verfassung und Verfassungsgebung. Zur Kritik des Theorems einer 'Emergenz' supranationaler und transnationaler Verfassungen." In *Staatliche Souveränität und transnationales Recht,* edited by Regina Kreide and Andreas Niederberger, 28–71. Mering bei Augsburg.

Mayer, Max Ernst. 1922. *Rechtsphilosophie*. Berlin.

Mazower, Mark. 2010. "Ende der Zivilisation und Aufstieg der Menschenrechte. Die konzeptionelle Trennung Mitte des 20. Jahrhunderts." In *Moralpolitik. Geschichte der Menschenrechte im 20. Jahrhundert,* edited by Stefan-Ludwig Hoffmann, 41–62. Göttingen.

Menke, Christoph, and Francesca Raimondi, eds. 2011. *Die Revolution der Menschenrechte. Grundlegende Texte zu einem neuen Begriff des Politischen*. Berlin.

Möllers, Christoph. 2005. *Gewaltengliederung. Legitimation und Dogmatik im nationalen und internationalen Rechtsvergleich*. Tübingen.

———. 2008. *Demokratie—Zumutungen und Versprechen*. Berlin.

———. 2008. *Die drei Gewalten. Legitimation der Gewaltengliederung in Verfassungsstaat, Europäischer Integration und Internationalisierung*. Weilerswist.

———. 2009. *Das Grundgesetz. Geschichte und Inhalt*. Munich.

Müller, Harald. 2008. *Wie kann eine neue Weltordnung aussehen? Wege in eine nachhaltige Politik*. Frankfurt am Main.

———. 2008. "Parlamentarisierung der Weltpolitik—Ein skeptischer Warnruf." In *Transnationale Verrechtlichung. Nationale Demokratien im Kontext globaler Politik*, edited by Regina Kreide, 137–59. Frankfurt / New York.

Müller, Jörg Paul. 2002. *Die demokratische Verfassung*. Zürich.

Niesen, Peter. 2001. "Volk-von-Teufeln-Republikanismus. Zur Frage nach den moralischen Ressourcen der liberalen Demokratie." In *Die Öffentlichkeit der Vernunft und die Vernunft der Öffentlichkeit. Festschrift für Jürgen Habermas*, edited by Klaus Günther and Lutz Wingert, 568–604. Frankfurt am Main.

———. 2002. "Legitimität ohne Moralität. Habermas und Maus über das Verhältnis zwischen Recht und Moral." In *Zwischen Recht und Moral. Neuere Ansätze der Rechts- und Demokratietheorie*, edited by Peter Niesen and René von Schomberg, 16–60. Münster.

———. 2008. "Deliberation ohne Demokratie? Zur Konstruktion von Legitimität jenseits des Nationalstaates." In *Transnationale Verrechtlichung. Nationale Demokratien im Kontext globaler Politik*, edited by Regina Kreide, 240–259. Frankfurt / New York.

Niesen, Peter, and Benjamin Herborth, eds. 2007. *Anarchie der kommunikativen Freiheit. Jürgen Habermas und die Theorie der internationalen Politik*. Frankfurt am Main.

Niesen, Peter, and René von Schomberg, eds. 2002. *Zwischen Recht und Moral. Neuere Ansätze der Rechts- und Demokratietheorie*. Münster.

Offe, Claus. 2007. "Rekonstruktion oder Dekonstruktion des 'Westens'?" In *Souveränität, Recht, Moral. Grundlagen politischer Gemeinschaft*, edited by Tine Stein, Hubertus Buchstein, and Claus Offe, 185–95. Frankfurt am Main/New York.

Paine, Thomas. 1995. *Rights of Man*. First published 1792. Oxford World Classics, New York.

Pelinka, Anton. 2002. "Die französische Revolution als Beginn der modernen Demokratieentwicklung." In *Die Französische Revolution und das Projekt der Moderne*, edited by Helmut Reinalter and Anton Pelinka, 217–21. Vienna.

Pendas, Devin O. 2010. "Auf dem Weg zu einem globalen Rechtssystem? Die Menschenrechte und das Scheitern des legalistischen Paradigmas des Krieges." In *Moralpolitik. Geschichte der Menschenrechte im 20. Jahrhundert*, edited by Stefan-Ludwig Hoffmann, 226–55. Göttingen.

Preuss, Ulrich K., ed. 1994. *Zum Begriff der Verfassung*. Frankfurt am Main.

Raimondi, Francesca. 2011. Introduction to Chapter 2, in *Die Revolution der Menschenrechte. Grundlegende Texte zu einem neuen Begriff des Politischen*, edited by Christoph Menke and Francesca Raimondi, 95–101. Berlin.

Reinalter, Helmut, and Anton Pelinka, eds. 2002. *Die Französische Revolution und das Projekt der Moderne*. Vienna.

Rifkin, Jeremy. 2005. *The European Dream. How Europe's Vision of the Future Is Quietly Eclipsing the American Dream*. New York.

Rödel, Ulrich, ed. 1990. *Autonome Gesellschaft und libertäre Demokratie*. Frankfurt am Main.

Rousseau, Jean-Jacques. 1977. *Vom Gesellschaftsvertrag oder Grundsätze des Staatsrechts* [Du Contrat Social (The Social Contract)], first published 1762, translated into German and edited by Hans Brockard, Stuttgart.

Ryffel, Hans. 1969. *Grundprobleme der Rechts- und Staatsphilosophie. Philosophische Anthropologie des Politischen*. Neuwied / Berlin.

———. 1972. "Zur Rolle des 'Absoluten' in der Philosophie der Politik." In *Mensch und Recht. Festschrift für Erik Wolf zum 70. Geburtstag*, edited by Alexander Hollerbach, Werner Maihofer, and Thomas Würtenberger, 28–56. Frankfurt am Main.

Sandkühler, Hans Jörg, ed. 2010. *Recht und Moral*. Hamburg.

———. 2010. "Moral und Recht? Recht oder Moral?" In *Recht und Moral*, edited by Hans Jörg Sandkühler, 9–32. Hamburg.

Schmidt, Thomas M. 2007. "Vernunftrecht und göttliche Gebote. Religion als vorpolitische Quelle der Menschenrechte?" In *Die Freiheit der Religion im europäischen Verfassungsrecht*, edited by Stefan Kadelbach and Parinas Parhisi, 15–27. Baden-Baden.

Schneider, Catherine. 2011. "Human Rights and Transfers of Sovereignty in the European Union: Consequences for the Definition and Development of Human Rights." In *Definition and Development of Human Rights and Popular Sovereignty in Europe*, edited by Council of Europe Publishing, 151–75. Strasbourg.

Schwartländer, Johannes, ed. 1978. *Menschenrechte. Aspekte ihrer Begründung und Verwirklichung*. Tübingen.

——. 1978. "Staatsbürgerliche und sittlich-institutionelle Menschenrechte." In *Menschenrechte. Aspekte ihrer Begründung und Verwirklichung*, edited by Johannes Schwartländer, 77–95. Tübingen.

Simitis, Spiros. 1989. "Die Lois Chapelier: Bemerkungen zur Geschichte und möglichen Wiederentdeckung des Individuums." *Kritische Justiz*: 157–75.

Stein, Tine, Hubertus Buchstein, and Claus Offe, eds. 2007. *Souveränität, Recht, Moral. Die Grundlagen politischer Gemeinschaft*. Frankfurt am Main / New York.

Thomann, Marcel. 1983. "Rechtsphilosophische und rechtsgeschichtliche Etappen der Idee der Menschenrechte im 17. und 18. Jahrhundert." In *Gerichtslaubenvorträge—zum 75. Geburtstag von Hans Thieme*, edited by K. Kroeschel, 73–83. Sigmaringen.

Ulrich, Peter. 2008. *Integrative Wirtschaftsethik. Grundlagen einer lebensdienlichen Ökonomie*, fourth printing, Bern / Stuttgart / Vienna.

Vosskuhle, Andreas. 2010. "Der europäische Verfassungsgerichtsverbund." *Neue Zeitschrift für Verwaltungsrecht* 1: 1–18.

Vossler, Otto. 1929. "Die amerikanischen Revolutionsideale in ihrem Verhältnis zu den europäischen." *Historische Zeitschrift* / Supplement 17.

———. 1930. "Studien zur Erklärung der Menschenrechte." *Historische Zeitschrift* 142: 516–545.

Wellmer, Albrecht. 1993. *Endspiele: Die unversöhnliche Moderne*. Frankfurt am Main.

Wesel, Uwe. 2010. *Geschichte des Rechts in Europa*. Munich.

_____. 2010. "Die neue Weltordnung," in *Die Zeit* (weekly paper), 25 July 2010.

Wolf, Klaus Dieter. 2011. "Unternehmer als Normunternehmer: Global Governance und das Gemeinwohl." In *Recht ohne Staat? Zur Normativität nichtstaatlicher Rechtsetzung*, edited by Stefan Kadelbach and Klaus Günther, 101–18. Frankfurt am Main / New York.

INDEX